Coming into Our Fullness

On Women Turning Forty

INTERVIEWS AND PHOTOGRAPHS BY
CATHLEEN ROUNTREE

FOREWORD BY RIANE EISLER

❋ The Crossing Press, Freedom, California 95109

In loving memory of Sierra,
the constant, steady heartbeat of my life.

Library of Congress Cataloging–in–Publication Data
Rountree, Cathleen.
    Coming into our fullness : on women turning forty : interviews and
photographs / by Cathleen Rountree.
        p.   cm.
    ISBN 0-89594-518-5 (cloth) — ISBN 0-89594-517-7 (paper)
    1. Middle aged women—United States—Interviews.   2. Midlife
crisis—United States.   I. Title.
HQ1059.5.U5R68 1991
305.4'084'4—dc20   91-25361
                                                          CIP

ACKNOWLEDGMENTS

The publishing of this book is an opportunity to thank those who have assisted me during the years it took to reach its completion. I extend my heartfelt gratitude to my publisher, Elaine Goldman Gill, and to the staff at Crossing Press.

Several friends read through my manuscript at various stages of its development. Thanks to Mary Mackey and Maurine Doerkin for their encouragement and for many hours of engaging discourse.

I sincerely thank each woman who participated in this project, for giving generously of her time and personal revelations. Their collective stories are colorful mosaics and through piecing them together I have been able to form a more accurate understanding of my own life. Not only would this book have been impossible without them, but my own labyrinthine journey would have been much less interesting and valuable. I am a fuller woman for having known them.

The actual work on this book lasted nearly five years, but those five years of writing were preceded by a lifetime of living. To my family I am forever indebted: my grandmother, who opened me to the world of my senses through food gathering, preparation and appreciation, and whose love rarely failed me as a child; my mother, Marilu A. Lindley, who taught me the art of personal cultivation; my father, Owen Lord MacGregor, who gave me life—twice; Sierra, who for thirteen years was my familiar, alter ego, Bodhisattva—may I personify his pure joy and true devotion; and most importantly to my son, Christian, whose company I most enjoy, and whose maturity and inherent depth of character are a perpetual source of learning for me. I would also like to thank Jana Bartko, a young woman wise beyond her years (who feels like family to me), for her genuine interest in my work and concern for my happiness. Knowing her makes life more fun.

Many friends have supported me (in every way imaginable) throughout my 42 years. I wish to give special thanks to the following: Daniel Mark Delaney, our enduring friendship has spanned thirty years of marriages and divorces (not to each other), births and deaths, and everything in between, and to his wife, Kalen; Pat Ward Zimmerman (aka: Sister Dorothy Clare when I first met her in 1962) as both my English and religion teacher in a Catholic girls' high school, who exploded my mind with existential philosophy and Jewish Mysticism. She is catholic in the true sense of the word. I owe her so much; Vicki Noble's profoundly generous friendship has often mirrored and lovingly encouraged my difficult but tenacious personal odyssey; Nancy Ashley taught me that attitude is everything and that when I altered my perceptions life seemed more eager to smile on me; Christiane Corbat, my friend whom I never see frequently enough, thank you for recognizing "The Emerging Crone." A very deep gratitude must be expressed to Alain Cohen who for many years supported and sustained my efforts toward fullness. His faith in my artistry and intelligence was genuine enough to make me a believer, at last.

I thank the following, all of whom offered their friendship over the years and contributed to my growth and well-being: Marc Newman for opening my mind as well as my heart; Julia Osborn and Alec Cast for helping me confront the paper dragon of my own fears; Michael Park and Kevin Connelly, and Diane Gysbers, my Topanga Canyon heart-connection; Deena Metzger for inducting me into the writing life, and for holding the through-line as I straddled both the visible and invisible worlds; Bronwyn Jones for her personal warmth and her professional assistance with this project mid-way through its completion; Erica Mann-Ramos for knowing my dream could come true; and to Ruth and Lloyd Morgan, Dan and Judy Phillips, Peter and Janie Eichorn, Gigi and Albert Benat, and Kathryn and Ashley James for their continued friendship over many cycles of life.

I especially wish to thank Hal Stone for his support, and his Voice Dialogue which offered me a new language to access and communicate with the many hidden aspects of myself. Natashia Heifitz has provided me with over 10 years of Trager body work—her move to Italy is California's loss. Arnold Mindell's work has been significant to me as has that of Joan Halifax and The Ojai Foundation, and the exemplary grace of Thich Nhat Hanh who introduced me to the practice of Mindfullness. The five years spent in Reichian Therapy with John Rinn were crucial to making friends with my body; and my work with Bob Hoffman in the Hoffman Process propelled me further along the path of self-knowledge.

During the last few months of the completion of this book several new friends entered my life: I thank Coeleen Kieber for her loving kindness during a period of extreme emotional duress; Dr. Beth Wilderman for her sensitive assistance with Sierra's passing; Gail Tager for meaty and amusing conversation over several lunches; Kimberly and Mima at Carried Away for providing me with food that is nurturing as well as nourishing; and the "No Limits" group in Berkeley, in particular Beth Grossman. Betsy Sharp was beyond efficient in her transcribing skills; and Jude Wagge printed many of the black and white photographs for this book from my negatives. I also thank Kris Ihli for his healing ways; and Ashby Armistead for sharing both his creative inspiration and confidence in me.

Nina Winter's book, *Interview With the Muse*, which I read in the late 1970s certainly planted the first seed for this book. I thank Nina Winter whose life and tragic death touched my own. Charlotte Painter's and Pamela Valois's *Gifts of Age* is a beautiful book that inspired *Coming into Our Fullness*. And, of course, I wish to thank Riane Eisler for her Foreword to my book.

▪ C O N T E N T S ▪

This book is dedicated, with love and gratitude,
to my son, Christian Wright

a time when women and men all over the world are taking a
t the scripts we were handed for our lives. Many of us are
write these scripts, revising them to fit our human needs,
and potentials.

en, one of the most important revisions deals with our
ge. In the old script, while men gain value with age (as in
of the wise old man), women lose it. In the new script,
the ancient archetype of the wise woman or crone) also
age.

Our Fullness focuses on turning forty as a rite of passage,
richer, more fulfilling life. It contains the stories of
them well-known and others less so, who have rewrit-
ts in creative and often amazing ways.

different stories, written by very different women,
s backgrounds, ages, races, professions, religions, and
avocations. But there is in all of them a common thread: the search for
self, for our own authentic and unique paths as women in a world where
gender stereotypes continue to constrict our life options.

They are beautiful stories, stories of strength and determination in
the face of great obstacles and even tragedies; stories of love unfettered
by conventional constraints; stories of compassion, creativity, and courage. Above all, they are stories that reclaim for us our power as women
to shape our own lives—and with this, our world.

This is why these are very important stories, providing materials for
life scripts that are appropriate for what in my work I have called a
partnership-oriented prehistory, when the crone (the aging and experienced woman) was not only an honored aspect of mortal women, but of
the Great Goddess herself.

As I was reading these stories, I kept thinking how for me as I grew
up in Vienna, in Cuba, and after the age of fourteen in the United
States, there were no such powerful female role models. In most of what

I read, men were the protagonists, with women relegated to secondary roles as wives, temptresses, daughters, mothers—and, in famous epics such as *The Odyssey* and the Arthurian legends, men's prizes for defeating their opponents in war. And even in the novels that I read as a child that had women protagonists—classics such as *Anna Karenina*, *Madame Bovary*, and *Jane Eyre*—women's lives were centered around men.

By and large, these heroines were obsessed with their male lovers or employers. Another great heroine, Joan of Arc, adopted the male role of the holy warrior. All these are hardly positive role models for the young girl trying to find herself. Even worse, as I now look back on these works that are still touted as great books, I see that their message is that women who dare to deviate from a female script that severely constricts women's life options will be punished. Indeed, I realize that these women did not even live to the age of forty!

The messages must have suggested to me that if I as a woman tried to find my own way in life, I too would probably die at a young age as a punishment for my "transgressions." And I almost did die during my forties. But that time, when everything seemed to be falling apart, brought a new strength, purpose, and meaning—and finally, a new integration.

It was not easy for me to rewrite my life script, and in my case it certainly took a great toll. But now that I am almost sixty years old, I see that had I not done that, I would have had to deal with another kind of death: the death of what I now most highly value: my creativity, my ability to take risks, and my passionate commitment to the creation of a more equitable and peaceful world. Moreover, had I not rewritten my life script, I would never have had the opportunity or strength to form the kind of relationship that I now have: a real partnership with a wonderful man—whom I met after the age of forty.

Still, I cannot help but think how much easier it would have been for me if I had had better role models. This is why I was so pleased when

Cathleen Rountree asked me to write the foreword for this beautiful book. I think we need thousands of books like this, if we are to counter the old dominator cultural messages, messages that in their devaluation of women and the so-called "feminine" (such as caring, non-violence, and empathy) not only deprive both women and men of satisfactory relations but also threaten our very survival as a planet.

It is my hope that many women and men will have the opportunity and pleasure of reading this book. For me it was like suddenly coming upon a mirror in which I could recognize myself, reflecting many of my own hopes, fears, experiences, struggles—and personal evolution. For that is ultimately what *Coming into Our Fullness* is about: our evolution as women and as human beings in a time that has been accurately described as one of both crisis and opportunity.

I have been deeply moved and greatly enriched by reading this book that so beautifully shows that the years after forty can be the most fruitful and fulfilling years of our lives. I hope that you will be too.

—Riane Eisler

(Riane Eisler is the author of the international best-seller *The Chalice and The Blade: Our History, Our Future*, and *The Partnership Way: New Tools for Living and Learning* (with social psychologist David Loye), co-founder of the Center for Partnership Studies in Pacific Grove, California.)

· I N T R O D U C T I O N ·

The coming of age portends all the freedoms men have always known and women never—mostly the freedom from fulfilling the needs of others and from being a female impersonator.
—Carolyn Heilbrun, *Writing a Woman's Life*

I turned forty on 7 July, 1988, and threw an elaborate birthday party for myself two days later. It was held in the Bay Area in order to accommodate my 19-year-old son, Christian, and many friends whom, with enormous guilt, I'd abandoned a few years earlier in order to follow my heart to Los Angeles.

During this eventful, complex weekend my fiancé and I decided to dissolve our increasingly difficult two-year relationship. It was the concluding chapter of my lifelong, rigidly held illusion that only a man, child, and home could provide for me the sense of security and belonging I'd never known. The poignancy lay in the fact that love, marriage, and family hadn't worked the first time, so what compelled me to repeat this delusion of romance, this "ronde," twenty years later?

Since childhood, I had been assured by the media of my privilege, indeed, my very *entitlement* to happiness through relationship and service to my family. As I turned forty, that lie was now exposed, the dream shattered.

Cocooning myself into a safe living situation, a womb in a beautiful and (as it turned out) healing, natural environment in the Santa Monica Mountains, I plunged into a journey of despair and personal transformation unknown to me before. What had brought me into this subjective confrontation was the physical and psychological isolation I felt. Both were heightened by living in Southern California's vast, alienating distances, teeming freeways, and omnipresent sexist billboards and ageist, youth–obsessed advertising.

Depression was certainly not new to me. Zora Neale Hurston had perfectly described the depressed state when she wrote, "A Cosmic loneliness was my constant shadow." It had appeared with such regularity as to fade my colorful life experiences into dismal black and white

1

still photographs. In the past I had frequently fallen unconscious, impaired by despair and hopelessness, unable to perform my daily tasks and activities as society required.

That autumn after my fortieth birthday I dreaded the coming of winter as if it foreshadowed my own death. These dark premonitions were not entirely without ground, for on the first day of October at exactly seven o'clock in the morning my maternal grandmother succumbed to heart(break)failure. It was the beginning of my dance with demons which was to become a marathon through the days and months to come.

Two weeks to the day after Grandma died, I began writing an essay about Marilyn Monroe, who held considerable fascination for me as America's image of the quintessential "woman." I simultaneously was reading Alice Miller's insightful and disturbing book *The Drama of the Gifted Child* and Gloria Steinem's *Marilyn/Norma Jeane*. I began to overlay Miller's theory of narcissistic disturbance on Monroe's life as detailed by Steinem. I did not do this intentionally, but in retrospect I recognize the ostensible signs of life's lucid and unmistakable guidance. According to Carolyn Heilbrun, "...women transform themselves only after an awakening. And that awakening is identifiable only in hindsight."

During this period of hindsight and acute introspection, I asked myself why I had woven and sustained an empathic bond with Marilyn Monroe in particular, a woman dead for over twenty five years. Through my ardent commitment to understand my own neglected childhood and to unravel the subsequent personal myths, I came to understand the formative childhood experiences and consequent personal myths of a legendary public figure named Marilyn Monroe.

Gloria Steinem called Monroe a "female impersonator," someone who pretends to be something she believes she is not. Her psyche was so obsessed with trying to be who she thought others wanted her to be that there was no genuine opportunity for inner exploration, for the full meeting with and embracing of the Self which alone, I now appreciate and understand, can bring peace and enduring contentment. This process of personal understanding and self-transformation is, in part, what *Coming into Our Fullness: On Women Turning Forty* is about.

Marilyn Monroe is a symbol, an archetype of the Bitch/Goddess with which every thinking/feeling woman is familiar. Her struggle for independence, recognition, equality, and a peaceful home within herself remains our struggle. Through psychotherapy and various Twelve Step Programs we are finding that the damage and horror of her scarred and sexually abused childhood is our own. While reading *Marilyn/Norma Jeane* I realized that we have Marilyn's aborted life as an example of what not to do with our own. It happened that the tragedy of her life and death, as well as that of another woman caught in a similar web of misery, the poet, Sylvia Plath, could be viewed as the beginning of the contemporary Women's Movement in the 1960s. Marilyn Monroe, along with Sylvia Plath and others, died before her fortieth birthday.

Through the work of courageous women in the '60s and '70s, we now live in a time when women openly provide support and nurturance for each other. We are also encouraged by this sisterhood to develop our uniqueness through our intrinsically spiritual natures and artistic talents.

During the course of my fortieth year I came face to face with my very own values. I have learned to move beyond the false belief that my worth is determined by how attractive a man finds me. The days of compromise are over. I have renounced the old way of love, the lure of being the object of male desire and the prisoner of the male gaze.

I am learning to live without a man as the center of my life, without orbiting around him. I seek the common bond of living and working together for a "Partnership Future" as described by Riane Eisler in her seminal books *The Chalice and the Blade* and *The Partnership Way*.

The women, herein, who tell their stories are by anyone's standards self-actualized women—role models of creativity, productive living, and personal authenticity. Each in her own way has been a teacher for me. Like them, I too am learning to become my own authority.

While our culture is almost wholly outer-directed and goal-oriented (we receive training solely in doing and none in simply being), these women bear a torch to pilot us to safer ground. They each have as the core of their lives a creative form and/or spiritual practice rather than an addiction to the empty, pop-cultural diversions that we habitually use to keep us from ourselves.

As members of a society in which we have been denied or have given up the dignity of our rites of passage, the women in this book have devised their own initiations into a productive middle life. They are transmuting the dreaded midlife crisis into a promising midlife discovery. Each is improvising her script as she lives it. Each is original, moving through uncharted territory; each has been tested and has shown great bravery, fortitude, and a deep passion for life and truth.

Lives are stories. It is a human need to give shape to things...to understand. Every woman's life is like a Biblical story or a cultural myth—a metaphor for our own existence. Every positive and negative experience can be used as a learning tool. The women on the following pages offered to me the most intimate narrative accounts of their interior lives.

Despite differences in culture, profession, social standing, and geography, we all participate in this female initiation into midlife without noticeable ritual. During my period of questioning and melancholia surrounding my fortieth year, I consciously reached out because of these concerns and shared my private experiences with other women. Together, I hoped, we would be able to discuss the effect of gravity on our bodies while simultaneously exalting in the freeing of our minds. I found extraordinary vigor and wisdom in the female voice.

Some of the women interviewed are intimate friends and were

4

chosen because they have been role models for me. Others are public figures whom I sought to interview because their work was already known in the world. I have a marked admiration and affection for them, and each woman is a gift in my life with an individual and particular effect on me. I focused upon women who were in their forties, because as each one agreed, there *is* a palpable change that can be only anticipated in the thirties.

The questions I asked these women primarily referred to issues in women's lives: creativity, love, sexuality, relationship, spirituality, hopes and fears, mothering, friends, work, vanity, intellectual development, purpose, success, major life influences, and happiness.

I found a vitality, a combination of playfulness and seriousness due, in part, to a newly acquired but penetrating cognizance of their physical mortality and to an enormous sense of responsibility to the rest of humanity and the environment. Again and again I heard the words, "There is no more time to waste."

The title, *Coming into Our Fullness: On Women Turning Forty*, expresses personal empowerment through mindful awareness, through self-knowledge, acceptance, and appreciation, and through a willingness and ability to share those attributes in healthy, loving ways with all other sentient beings. As Thich Nhat Hanh, the well-known and venerated Vietnamese Zen Buddhist monk, says, "There is no way to happiness, happiness *is* the way." Every woman I interviewed has understood this maxim and incorporated it into a daily philosophy and practice.

Many of us spent our first twenty years learning the ways of the wounded; the next twenty were spent healing those wounds. The healings took innumerable twists and turns. Now, turning forty, we've begun to weave together painful experience and joyful expression into a certain balance, an evenness.

The truth often hurts and finding one's own truth seems, inevitably, to be a painful journey. But as Phyllis Old Dog Cross, a mental health

5

nurse consultant for the Indian Health Services once said:

> Each woman has an inner strength that she must find; only she can help herself through contemplative ways. When a person has achieved spiritual strength, she can do anything she wants.

Daily we are assaulted with the signs of the times, the ultimate collapse of the present system (ecological, political, economic, cultural, family) as we know it. We have lived through the extreme '50s and '60s, the excess and indulgence of the '70s and '80s and are tenuously navigating our future into the '90s, into the 21st century. The world is ripe for evolutionary transformation. The women I interviewed personify the universal human yearnings for an unprecedented future: a future of self-realization and planetary peace.

Each woman who crosses the threshold of forty can greet it with the wit and wisdom of her accumulated life experiences, and snake dance into a celebration of her unique existence, albeit sometimes tempered and bittersweet. We no longer need live with the damaging stereotypes of aging, as did Marilyn, no longer devote our lives to fulfilling the demands of the nuclear family, no longer live our lives as "female impersonators" or "performance artists."

Does life begin at forty? As Deena Metzger, poet and novelist disclosed during our interview:

> It really does get better. Love is better, sex is better, there's more intelligence, more heart, more warmth, much more contact with myself, deeper knowing of myself, as I get older. And I have such appreciation of the world we've been given.

Based on my own experiences, the lives of others, and a review of fiction and scholarship about midlife, I am convinced that the second half of a woman's life is a profound opportunity for transformation.

Aptos, California
May, 1991

6

Dear Sisters, please remember:
The jewel
Is in your bosom;
Why look for it
Somewhere
Else?

—Japanese Folk Zen Saying

I've always felt proud of my age. I think people should be proud that they've been around long enough to have learned something.

—Frances Moore Lappé

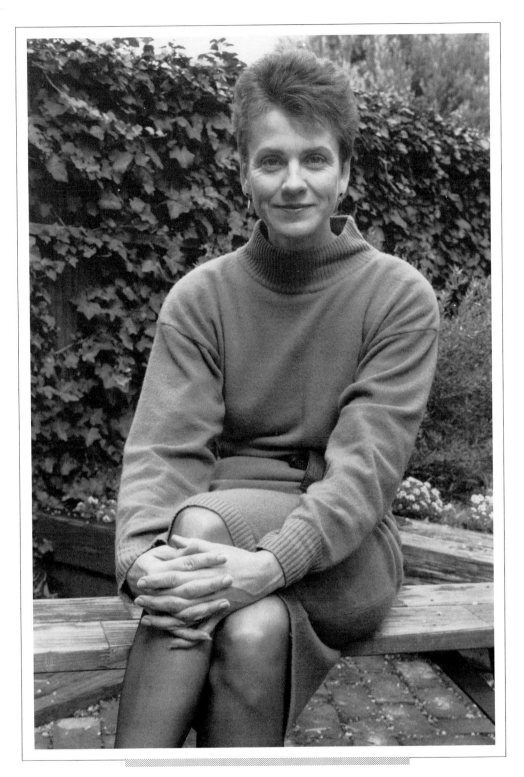

Frances Moore Lappé

I was perplexed by the appearance of the woman who opened the door at the Institute for the Arts of Democracy: she seemed demure and suburban. "So this is the woman, the *cause célèbre*, who single-handedly changed the way in which people worldwide view the politics of food," I thought. Later during our discussion Frances Moore Lappé revealed that she likes to shock people with her "ordinariness" so that they may more easily identify with her and therefore believe they too can change the world. It works.

Diet for a Small Planet, Lappé's first book, published in 1971, provoked a questioning of the accepted views of American food production and consumption that, twenty years and three *million* copies later, continues to be relevant. Recognizing that overwhelming social problems, especially global ones such as world hunger and ecological destruction, paralyze us, she used food as the entry point for developing solutions to the world's problems.

Her original premise was that what every individual eats is within our control, yet the act ties us to the economic, political, and ecological order of our entire planet. According to Frances much of what we grew up believing about a healthy diet is false. Even a seemingly small change—consciously choosing a diet that is good for both our bodies and for the Earth—can lead to a series of choices that will transform all of our lives.

Frances has devoted her life to problem solving and has most recently launched the Institute for the Arts of Democracy with her soon-to-be husband, Paul DuBois. According to Frances, "As long as democracy remains merely a set of formal institutions, we cannot meet the unprecedented challenges of our time. Democracy must become not what we 'have' but what we 'do'— *democracy as a way of life* built on the capacities of ordinary citizens and drawing forth our passion and participation. We call it citizen democracy."

It was in her mid-forties that Frances met her partner Paul, with whom she feels she will live and work for the rest of her life. This relationship has been the most joyful in her experience and she believes that is because it began as a friendship: "We discovered a level of communication between two friends before there was any romance or any thought of a life partner. That's a powerful lesson that took me a long time to learn."

Having raised two children, Anthony and Anna, mostly as a single mother, Frances describes them as "the grounding force" in her life. In *Diet for a Small Planet* she lovingly wrote, "They keep me from working so hard that I would run the risk of burning out. They pull me back from feelings of despair. They are positive. They welcome each day. With people like that around, no wonder I have energy."

I'm not surprised when she smiles and tells me the three of them remain close even though they have both left home to attend college.

Throughout the course of my interview with her, Frances was both earnest about implementing action for social reform and eager to share her methods. Although she doesn't believe that people are born optimistic, she feels that continual growth and change are crucial in order to cultivate hope. She maintains the youthful enthusiasm of the high school cheerleader she once was. Only now the stakes for peace, abundance, and citizen democracy are considerably higher.

▪ FRANCES MOORE LAPPÉ ▪

I grew up in Fort Worth, Texas, in the '50s. The most formative part of my childhood had to do with my parents' avocation rather than their work. They founded a Unitarian Church with their friends in the 1940s. The family story goes that I came home from Baptist Sunday school and said, "Mommy, what does hellfire and brimstone mean?" They said, "Oh, my God!" and immediately put an ad in the paper for anybody interested in a Unitarian fellowship. Co-founding Food First and the Institute for the Arts of Democracy always struck me as very similar to what they were trying to do in founding the church. I see many parallels. The church was a place for people to come together and bring their private values and aspirations into the public world. Many of the principles of Unitarianism had to do with everything that my current work is trying to embody.

I lived a dual life, because through my parents' influence I was involved with one set of values: they actively opposed racist policies and believed in bringing people together to solve common problems through the democratic process. Their example helped me to develop an inner life. And, yet, my high school was a very racist environment. There wasn't any intellectual or protest subculture at that time. I was a cheer-leader and dated the football captain. That was my visible life in high school. Living these two lives was extremely uncomfortable, but I survived. I was just waiting to get out of Texas. I was one of the few kids from my high school who went to college, much less left the state.

My first goal in life was to be a diplomat and save the world through the U.S. State Department, so I went to American University's School of International Service in Washington D.C. I was disillusioned with the program. It was very hard-nosed in its approach, "America First." I ended up going someplace that was just the opposite—a small Quaker college in the Midwest, Earlham College.

During my senior year I was utterly distraught by the Vietnam war and became very involved in anti-war work. I was a fanatic. I admit it. I regarded anybody not working against the war as immoral. I applied to go to Vietnam to do reparations work with a voluntary service, but I wasn't accepted. I decided that the problem was in our *own* society and that I had to focus on what I could do here.

So I moved to Philadelphia—this was during the War on Poverty and the Model Cities Program—and became part of the Neighborhood Renewal Project, a federally funded urban development program. My job was to work with people in low-income units and to organize welfare recipients into self-help networks. Soon, I realized that even if I were to succeed every day in what I was doing, it really wouldn't address the causes of the problems. I also felt uncomfortable being the "organizer behind the scenes," putting other people on the line taking risks, when I knew I could always come home to a comfortable apartment.

During this time I married an aspiring young scientist, Marc Lappé. We eventually moved to Berkeley, California where he was in cancer research at the University. I enrolled in the community organizing program in the graduate program of the social work school. Still, I remained frustrated because I didn't know how what I was doing related to the underlying causes of people's pain. So I dropped out in the spring of '69. I made the decision that most changed my life. I stopped. I decided not to do anything until I knew why what I was doing mattered— why I was choosing one path as opposed to another path—and how it related to understanding causes of people's suffering that seemed so needless. I felt that I had to discover something that was true to me, even if it didn't go anywhere. It was either that chosen life or one of misery.

I was terrified that I didn't have a direction, didn't have a label. My husband was a brilliant young scientist and a Ph.D., teaching courses on Chinese Philosophy and Ecology at the Free University at Berkeley, and I had no idea what I was doing! So I spent the next year auditing courses, going to lectures, taking notes, and retreating, trying to figure out where I was headed. I was trying to educate myself, though I had no idea that I was going to be a writer.

This was during the time of the budding global consciousness, and I was reading such books as Paul Ehrlich's *The Population Bomb*, which documents the limits to our resources. I was gripped by the concept that famine was inevitable. I wanted to find out the answers for myself. I met people who were interested in natural foods and consequently was becoming more aware of what I was eating. So I gravitated toward food early in that self-directed learning process. I read everything from textbooks to newspaper articles, anything I could find on the world's food problem.

What caught my imagination so early on was the realization that a great deal of information on this subject existed, but there was an enormous gap between what was available in research documents put out by official government and U.N. organizations, and what ordinary people knew. That was one of the motivations that kept me going—I wanted to share what I was learning with other people.

I began by writing a one-page handout just to share with friends. Soon it became a little booklet. That booklet came into the hands of the owners of Ballantine Books—then book companies were owned by real people, not huge conglomerates. Their son was a vegetarian; so immediately they were attracted to publishing *Diet for a Small Planet*. That fact alone changed my life. I was shocked by the book's success. I guessed it might appeal to about 500 people in the Greater Bay Area. I presumed the interest in natural foods was a fad that would peak in the early '70s. I thought what I was saying was so obvious. If it were correct, I figured, then the "experts" would have been saying it. I had a profound fear that I'd missed something, maybe I'd left out two zeros in some calculation or made some illogical leap and not even realized my error! But the book was taken seriously. In fact, I hadn't made any mistakes, I'd really done my homework. It was accurate and the book is still being used, even in medical schools, still selling well after twenty years.

The experience demystified the process of learning for me. After that, I felt I could learn whatever I needed to know, to say with some sense of confidence whatever I needed to say. In a sense this realization is what I've been trying to communicate to people ever since then. Much of my public speaking and relating to people now, particularly young people, is to shock them with my ordinariness, with the realization that I am just like them. So if I'm an expert, then they also can go out and dig up their own facts and become experts too.

After *Diet for A Small Planet* came out in '71, I had two kids and focused mainly on raising them. I really loved that time in my life and felt so happy in my supportive marriage and with my children. By the time my daughter was weaned and over two years old and becoming less dependent on me, I began to feel frustrated. I realized that because of *Diet for a Small Planet* I had a platform, but I didn't know what to do with it. I sank into a deep depression, thinking, "I have a solid platform from which I can now speak, and yet I'm not any clearer about where I'm headed."

The next year, the fall of 1974, I went to the World Food Conference in Rome. That was the first big international confab to devise a blueprint to end world hunger. I attended and became very motivated, ironically, by seeing the dearth of wisdom. I saw the authorities locked into the precise mindsets that were making problems worse.

Soon after, I met Joseph Collins at a conference at the University of Michigan. He was interested in writing a book on world hunger. Within six weeks of deciding to work together we had a $75,000 contract with Ballantine to write *Food First*. We put the money into founding the Institute for Food and Development Policy. Within a year I realized that I couldn't be an institute builder and public speaker and writer and mother and still be married. My feelings, I'm sure, reflected in part the era—the '70s—when there was a great deal of questioning the whole institution of marriage.

After my marriage ended, I was heavily involved in building the Institute. It is an educational center on the roots of hunger, although its role has always been broader than that. You can't talk about hunger without talking about every other major social problem. Through the Institute I was trying to help people cut through disempowering popular myths about hunger: that overpopulation is the simple cause or that better technology is the simple answer. I wrote about ten books on foreign policy and development while I was there—including how-to manuals for action against world hunger.

I married my second husband in 1985 and we had a commuting marriage because he lived in Wisconsin while I remained in California. We were together every summer and over holidays; I traveled there every month for six years to visit him. I love Wisconsin. We had a small cabin with a pond, totally private and beautiful—a cozy little love nest. The first year that worked for me because my children stayed with their father in California when I went to Wisconsin. Then my first husband moved to Chicago and I wasn't able to have that same peace of mind when I left them. I had them each going to the homes of various friends, but it never felt very comfortable. So that put additional strain on the whole situation. It was a pull that I hadn't anticipated when we got married. We finally cried "uncle."

Since 1976 I've been completely independent in terms of finances and house-buying and car-buying. In fact, marrying Paul will be the first time in fifteen years that I will have a partner in all that. My God, I never appreciated the stress that making all those choices can entail. In 1981, when I sold my house in San Francisco and bought the house in Oakland in order to keep my children near their father, I got shingles just from the stress of making all the decisions by myself. This will be the first time that I've had a full partner in fifteen years. What a luxury. I feel so spoiled now.

Paul and I are launching the Institute for the Arts of Democracy. The popular name that we use is Building Citizen Democracy. The point of that name is to suggest that democracy is not a formal structure of government. In fact, you can have all the beautiful constitutions in the world along with multiple parties and secret ballots and yet, still be missing true democracy. Democracy means people really having a voice and being able to express their values in public life. You can have the trappings of democracy, the formal shape of democracy, but not its heart and soul: people feeling, knowing, and actually exercising their capacities to voice their opinions and hold decision makers accountable.

So the "Arts of Democracy" suggests that creating this heart and soul is an art. *We're not born citizens.* To be effective in public life is something we have to develop over a lifetime. Our philosophy is that democracy is *a way of life*. The purpose of the Institute is to infuse this understanding into every aspect of every sector in our society that shapes people's conception of and participation in public life, to move our understanding away from thinking of democracy as something somebody else does up there, or something that is simply taken care of by the market or by formal laws that we take no responsibility for. We want to promote democracy as a way of life that is engaging and rewarding, difficult and challenging, and absolutely vital to developing our innate capacities as human beings.

Today people feel that public life is demeaning, demoralizing and ineffective. The more people feel that way, the more they withdraw, the more disappointing public life gets and the more it is taken over by very narrow interests and mean-spirited people. We want to figure out every way to break into the vicious cycle, to start to create public life as a rewarding arena of life.

We are just beginning to develop a strategy that has to do with analyzing the primary barriers to people's involvement. Part of it is at the belief system level. We have no model of citizen democracy. It doesn't exist anywhere. We want to help people see in their mind's eye a democracy that is richer, more vital and rewarding, by telling stories of the seeds of it that we now see emerging. We humans need to be able to "see" the future to create it. Our first project (a book called *Doing Democracy*) will take the themes that I've mentioned and use real people telling real stories to show that it's not just a pipe dream, that there are seedlings, if you will, that we can nourish.

Even though world problems seem more desperate, I personally feel more hopeful. I think today there is a more genuine search by more people, a genuine willingness to admit that we don't have simple answers. I find that very hopeful. There's a palpable searching that I didn't feel twenty years ago. The government is only a vehicle of what its citizens want, and we've got to find our voice. That probably means taking on more responsibility than we thought we could.

There are so many openings that didn't exist twenty years ago. Because of the environmental crisis, people are becoming aware of the interconnectedness of our global problems. It's harder to compartmentalize when you're aware of pollution and the general decline in the quality of life. How can the quality of your life be good if the roads are clogged, the public schools are a mess, there is crime on the streets, and the air is polluted? These problems affect everyone. Our fates are linked.

I don't think anyone is born optimistic or hopeful. Hope has to be cultivated. I think people are only hopeful when they are doing something in their lives that's making them change. I've always thought that you have to earn hope by continuing to grow and change. Then it builds on itself.

I made a conscious decision when I turned forty that my forties would be a transitional decade. My goal was that by the time I was fifty I would have made a transition. I had a hard time articulating exactly what that transition was, but it had to do with leaving behind the *Diet for a Small Planet* identity, narrowly focused on food, and moving to a larger public role addressing underlying values. I was determined not to be consigned to a particular issue but to address the larger underlying question, the social structure of democracy.

I felt that people needed more from me than just to be the critic. Yet I knew that I didn't want to invent another "ism." So what do you do? How do you offer hope and a solution without falling into the trap of promoting another dogma? I always saw my forties as a time of tremendous change, a transition in my life. And it has sure turned out that way!

Now I feel that, in the second half of my adult life, I want to build on my strengths and stretch myself, but in different ways. In building on my strengths I let go of feeling like I have to fill in all the weaknesses. I decided that by middle age maybe some things about me are never going to fundamentally change. It just seems silly to go on the rest of my life trying to change inhibitions and fears which are that deep in me. I want to put my energies in developing what I most have to offer. Also I want to draw people to me who energize me, whereas before I felt a duty that no matter how uncomfortable a relationship was I had to continue it. I want to work with people who are life-giving and whom I learn from. The motto at our institute is "It's Gotta Be Fun."

It seems obvious that if I'm talking about making public life rewarding for others, I've got to model that, showing people that it's rewarding for me. If I'm stressed and haggard–looking and overwhelmed by the magnitude of everything, how can I tell people that public life is something we can all find reward and joy in? I've got to be an honest person; I've got to have joy in my own life.

I have always felt proud of my age. In speeches I often throw in something that tells people what my age is. I do that very consciously. I've always thought you should be proud that you've been around long enough to have learned something and long enough to have had a variety of experience. So much has gotten easier for me being older. I so appreciate the road I've traveled and the lessons I've learned, and the realization that I don't have to repeat them.

This relationship with Paul has been the most joyful of my life, and it began as a friendship. We discovered a level of communication that was the deepest level of communication between two friends I'd ever experienced—before there was any romance or any thought of a life partner. That was a lesson that took me a long time to learn. It's what gives me absolute confidence in this marriage. There was no honeymoon. And if you don't have a honeymoon, then you have nothing to come down from—it just gets deeper and deeper. What gives me great calm and confidence is the core of fundamental respect we have, based on friendship. It's not respect based on my romantic dream of what I want this person to be for me. That's a powerful lesson I had to learn. There is such a contrast between who I am now, with who I was in my earlier marriages. I know myself better. I have much more to give.

I think wisdom is being able to analyze precisely where one's gifts intersect in a very precise way with what the world needs. It means doing that and not beating yourself up and fretting about all the other things you're not doing. I hope I am getting closer to that definition of wisdom.

I think of aging as a time when you can be more genuine, because you've earned it, you've paid your dues, you can care less about superficial impressions and just go for it, whatever you really want to do. Age can give you freedom and a greater confidence in living. But my greatest reward is the feeling of looking forward to the final half of my adult life, knowing I'm not starting from scratch, that I have a platform of real knowledge about the world, of contacts with people who know me. Therefore I can go into certain settings and have credibility. It's taken twenty-five years to build it. Now I'm carrying credibility from one field into another field. I'm moving from political economy to political philosophy, from economic analysis to social organizing. That's a pretty big shift. ■

Between twenty and forty is when you build all your connections, you build your base. It's at forty that you really come into your maturity as an artist.

—Judy Chicago

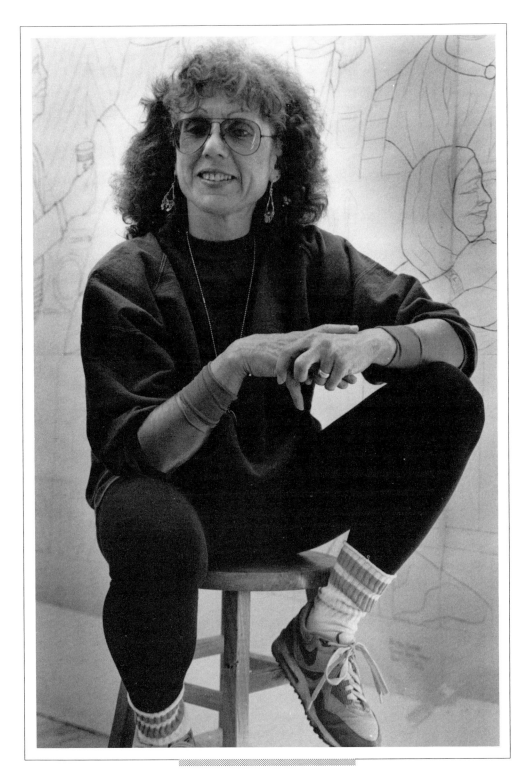

Judy Chicago

Known for her directness, Judy Chicago can be impatient with those who move at a more contemplative pace—either physically or intellectually. I felt apprehensive when I entered her home/office/studio in Santa Fe, New Mexico, where she was giving hell to someone on the telephone. After she hung up I was relieved to meet a woman who in person was less threatening than she sounded and in fact was quite friendly. Short and compact, with an athlete's bearing, Judy Chicago was an explosion of color: a fireball of red/orange hair, over-sized mauve glasses, purple sweatshirt, and fuschia turtleneck. And she has the inexhaustible energy to match. That energy is exponentially increased through her devotion to physical exercise and her passion for creating art, and her love for her husband, Donald Woodman, and their five cats.

After a tour of the artist's adobe studio, in which she is working on large-scale paintings (including two works for stained glass) for her current undertaking, *The Holocaust Project*, we squeezed into the breakfast room—barely large enough to house one circular glass table, four chairs and three huge cats. Judy was set against a field of light in the window created by the afternoon sun. It equaled her personal warmth and dynamism.

Her words spoke of hope, but sorrow is engraved on her face, and grief is etched in the eyes behind the rose-colored glasses. She is haunted by tragic events, both personal and collective.

Born Judy Cohen in her namesake, Chicago, Illinois, and descended from a line of twenty-three generations of rabbis, Judy Chicago believes that a strong sense of social values and intellectual curiosity was bred into her. Although raised in an assimilated family, she is proud of her Jewish ancestry, and exploring her Jewish heritage has recently become more compelling in her life and art.

Judy Chicago is arguably the foremost feminist artist in America today. Certainly she is one of the most controversial. With each art project she probes deeper into an exploration of the human experience. *The Dinner Party* (which was first exhibited when she was forty) rediscovered and celebrated historical women who contributed to Western civilization (among them saints, scientists, artists, and writers), many of whom have been eclipsed from our collective memory.

Later, Judy, who is childless, created *The Birth Project* in an attempt to fill a gap in Western art with images celebrating birth and creation. It originally evolved from her fascination with creation myths. "The idea that a male God created man is such a reversal of the reality of how life comes forth." The result was a view of birth as a metaphor for creation itself—for female production rather than reproduction. Lucy Lippard, the highly respected art critic, said of *The Birth Project*, "Chicago wanted to show that you can make 'fine art' with 'minor art,' that you can paint with thread, and she has succeeded. The formal inventiveness, the variety of color and line, the juxtapositions of different materials and textures are truly spectacular." Through *The Dinner Party* and *The Birth Project* Judy introduced women's experiences into the arts, and in so doing affirmed those experiences. Her commitment as an artist has always been to human values and the power art has to influence change.

Perhaps one of the most extraordinary aspects of Judy Chicago's work is the synthesis of her collaborative efforts with her own work. She often works in concert with other artisans, utilizing a number of techniques such as needlework, ceramics, china painting, and stained glass, which have traditionally been considered crafts.

The artist's current project on the Holocaust, done in collaboration with her photographer husband, Donald Woodman, will open in 1993 in Chicago, Illinois, at the Spertus Museum. The work has been in process since 1985. Judy feels that there is no major philosophical or feminist overview of the Holocaust in contemporary art. She is attempting to create a visual examination of the Holocaust and to illuminate the connections between racism and sexism. The images are gender-balanced, expressing the experience of both women and men. Their goal is to reach a wide and diverse audience and to stimulate dialogue that can contribute to a transformation in consciousness—a transformation that may help prevent the recurrence of another event like the Holocaust.

JUDY CHICAGO

I came from an assimilated Jewish family. My parents broke away from the old world and its traditions, and passed little information about Jewish identity or history on to me. However, because I come from a line of twenty-three rabbis, I was raised with a tremendous sense of Jewish ethics. That has probably shaped me.

I was brought up in a political household. My father believed in equal rights for women, and I saw women participate in discussions from the time I was a child. My mother worked; my father and my mother both raised me. I was a precocious child, started drawing at three, and began art school at five. My father died when I was thirteen; it was very traumatic. I left home at seventeen and went to California to go to college at UCLA, and was the first art major to graduate Phi Beta Kappa, because, unlike most other students, I had a humanities minor.

I had a feminist consciousness very early. I understood that some of what was happening to me was because I was female. I was always intellectually curious and took a class on the intellectual history of Europe. The professor said he would talk about women's contribution to European intellectual history at the end of the class. I waited and waited for the last session. The professor walked in, turned to the class, and said, "Women's contribution to European intellectual history: They made none!" and walked out. I'll never forget it. I was nineteen or twenty years old, and I flipped. I was so upset. I felt like a freak because I wanted to participate in culture, to be an artist, to enter history. I suppose that had something to do with my later inquiry into women's history, to find out if his theory was true.

I was raised with a reverence for the truth. That's probably what has kept me going, because no matter how hard things are, truth makes life bearable for me. The truth is comforting, even though it isolates me from many people who practice denial.

The Holocaust Project is an investigation of the conditions out of which the Holocaust originally grew and can grow again because anti–Semitism is still with us. My cousin traced back our lineage on my paternal grandmother and grandfather's side to a famous rabbi from Lithuania. Many Latvians and Lithuanians complied with the Nazis during the Holocaust. The major centers of Vilnius and Latvia were forty to fifty percent Jewish before the Holocaust, and now there is nothing, not even a memory.

Donald and I started out with the idea of commemorating the Jewish experience of the Holocaust, but, as we went along, our thinking changed and we began to make connections between the Holocaust and other examples of mass victimization. There really isn't any large body of art on the Holocaust. There is some in the Jewish community, but not in the larger art community and I am always attracted to voids, to subjects about which there is silence, as I think it allows for new thinking.

The Dinner Party was first exhibited when I was around forty. That initial showing in San Francisco was a huge success, but afterward other museums refused to show it. I thought that if I did a work of art that was successful—one hundred thousand people came to see it, it attracted the media, and balanced the museum's budget—I would probably get some opportunities. I thought other museums would want to show my work, that it would produce new opportunities in my career, but it didn't. On the contrary, I lost everything as a result of *The Dinner Party*: my marriage, my studio, my staff, everything. And I had to start all over again from scratch. For a year *The Dinner Party* wasn't shown. Eventually it was shown as a result of grass roots organizations around the country and then around the world. It turned out to be a triumph, and that was wonderful. *The Dinner Party* was seen by one million people. It was an amazing story and was, I think, unheard of in the art world. Life is full of contradictions and that's what makes it interesting.

I am most concerned that my contribution to art and culture be acknowledged and not wiped out of history. That's not what I anticipated would happen when I turned fifty. I did not expect that I would be threatened with becoming "the fortieth plate on *The Dinner Party* table," having everything I'd worked for become obscured or lost. I actually think that could happen. We still haven't reached the point at which we can ensure that the work women do will be preserved. All four of my books are out of print, *The Dinner Party* is in storage after it encountered an enormous assault that prevented it from being permanently housed. My work is still quite marginalized in the art world. That upsets me. There's greater recognition of what I've done *outside* my field than in it. There are many references to me and my work in literature, sociology, anthropology, history, several fields other than art.

But I think you have to remain hopeful, because at a certain point one has to make a choice philosophically. Who knows what is going to happen if I live thirty more years? And after all, the world will continue long after I'm gone. Maybe I'll be "discovered" by someone who, like me, questions what women did in the past. I don't know what the future holds. I choose to believe we have the capacity to transform ourselves as human beings. This makes life worth living, along with the joy of being with my husband, Donald, and trying to have a little fun and making art which gives the most meaning to my life.

This is my third marriage. I keep saying, "Three is a charm." Donald's not exactly the reward I expected to get, but he's the reward I got! I'm very happy to be married to him, and I think he feels the same way. Being intimate with another person is a wonderful antidote to despair; it's a way of making life in the present worth living. My voyage has led me to places of enormous despair, so I cherish the joy. As you get older things happen to you and around you: death, sickness, illness; and it's nice to have someone to face them with. We've had a great deal to face in the five years we've been together.

I know many women who delayed personal fulfillment and growth by giving up everything for twenty years. They married and gave up their lives to their husbands and their children and then one day woke up and said, "Fuck this!" Then they went through a major transformation. My life is not like that; I've had a consistent life for thirty years. I've worked mostly in my studio. I've spent a great deal of time thinking and addressing the issues that were of interest to me and doing the things I wanted to do. I don't spend much time thinking about what I might have done, because I did what I wanted to do. Basically I've been in charge of my life for a long time. I think most women are at the mercy of their lives. Whatever happens around them impacts upon them—if someone gets sick, or is needy, if someone comes to visit—whatever they're doing goes down the tubes. They are in service to the people around them. That's not how I live my life.

I would say to these women that there is an enormous payoff in terms of taking risks, standing up in the world, and facing it with courage. And the payoff is self–esteem. What I learned early in my life is that you don't have anything else in your life but yourself. Everything else is an illusion. You can lose your husband, home, security, friends, and children. All you have is yourself, and how you feel about yourself shapes your life, and whether it is going to be meaningful to you—or to anyone else! So if you give yourself away, you don't have much left.

Women are encouraged by pressure from society to give themselves away. My office journal shows how many requests come in every week for me to give myself up, give away my time, my work, my energy, my ideas—give, give, give; there are hardly any entries in the journal of anyone calling and wanting to give something *to me*: an opportunity, money, help, wanting to buy a piece of work. The perception that a woman is supposed to give all the time is unbelievably lopsided. And a successful woman is supposed to give even more! People don't understand how precarious my existence is financially. I own no property. I have absolutely no economic security after thirty years of work, none whatsoever. Through the Flower Corporation has evolved over the years, and is now the only support structure I have.

The Dinner Party is symbolic of women's history. If we lose our history again, how long will it be until the time and circumstances come together in which it can be pieced together? Between me and Christine de Pisan there were 500 years. She wrote *The Book of the City of Ladies* in the 15th century, in which she discovered all these women (probably rediscovered for the fifteenth time!)—all the women I rediscovered 500 years later. To lose them again is to regress terribly. I don't think women have really grasped the significance of this.

I studied the lives of other creative women, and saw which women had children and which ones didn't. I said to myself, "I'm not gonna be like the women who gave up their creative lives in order to have kids." I knew if Virginia Woolf and Georgia O'Keeffe and Anaïs Nin couldn't do it, why should I think *I* could? So I patterned myself after women who had succeeded in creating.

One of the things that's extremely frustrating to me is to see how young women refuse to accept information from older women. I did it too. I find it ironic. I understand from my own experience the way in which young women are encouraged to disconnect from older women, rather than to build on their experiences. Now young women are coming to me and it's wonderful to be able to pass on my experience, and it's great for them to be able to build on what I and other women have done, without giving up twenty years like countless women did before they clicked in. If those women had been properly educated, they would have started right out at twenty, not at forty. Between twenty and forty is when you build all your connections, you build your base. It's at forty that you really come into your maturity as an artist.

There's a payoff in life for everything. You get older and uglier, and your life gets deeper and richer. Gravity happens, and wrinkles and tiredness happen. You can face it with humor and a determination to struggle to keep it together, to keep going, and to wake up every morning with joy. You can do that, but it doesn't change the inherent difficulty in growing old. When you look at someone very old and feeble and sick, it's frightening, because you know it's coming. Not many people get the pleasure of dying peacefully in their sleep. Life is hard.

I don't want to live longer than I can be active: physically, aesthetically, sexually. I'm such a physical person that I don't know if I would want to be enfeebled. It will also depend on whether Donald were still alive, and if we could continue to have fun together. If I had my pal, my companion, I could imagine living into my eighties. I don't know if I want to live any longer than that. (Although the potter, Beatrice Wood, who's in her late nineties, is a great role model for an active and healthy old age.) Now that I really understand the nature of the world, I have a lot of grief. One of the things the Holocaust has taught me is either you get up and keep going, or you lie down and die; there aren't many alternatives. It's not in my nature to give up. I don't think it's in my lineage, either. ■

My marriage broke up in my forties, but I have to say I probably feel better about myself now than ever before, because I didn't break after my divorce. Something happened inside me: I came out the other side of despair.

—Ina Lea Meibach

Ina Lea Meibach

▪ P R O F I L E ▪

Raised in a sheltered Orthodox Jewish family in Brooklyn and the Bronx, Ina Lea Meibach's description of herself as a "real New Yorker" is fitting. Her life may have been guided by divine intervention (or, at least, very good luck) on several occasions, but she consciously maximized every opportunity. Ina attended a gifted girls' school, Hunter High, which she remembers was "like *The Prime of Miss Jean Brody*," a unique place where "the only thing everybody had in common was that they were all bright." There was a range in social status from debutantes and U.N. ambassadors' daughters to "kids who were given carfare for school." Her eyes lit up when she recalled that "the city of *Manhattan itself* was our school. Hunter was the best education I ever received. The whole world opened up to me. She had been so well educated at Hunter High that "by comparison, college was like playing." She pledged to the premier Jewish sorority and dove into a whirling social life.

Through the influence of her mother's closest friend, Ina entered law school at N.Y.U. and became a lawyer. Several twists and turns in the course of her life led her to the entertainment industry, where, at that time, she was "the only woman in the business." Ina Meibach soon became known as the "Rock Lawyer," and when people needed an attorney and couldn't think of anyone, they'd say, "What about that redhead?" She has represented many well-known rock groups over the years: The Who, Patti Smith, U2, Joe Jackson, Janis Ian, LaBelle, and Sinéad O'Connor.

Several success stories (in the form of gold, platinum, and silver records) are written on the walls of Ina's Fifth Avenue suite of offices (around the corner from the Museum of Modern Art) where she is the senior partner of Meibach, Epstein, Reiss and Regis. They are a testament to her durability in a fickle business. When I entered her private office, I was greeted by an ebullient, personable woman dressed elegantly in a turquoise, tailored wool jacket over a black wool skirt. Her flame-red hair blazed around her face, complementing her green eyes. We sat in her office for nearly three hours discussing everything from *peristroika* to the possible hoax of Jim Morrison's death. (She thinks he's still alive.)

As the narrative of her life unfolded, I was often surprised by the diversity of her experiences. It seemed that the phrase, "being in the right place at the right time" applied to her—with the exception of one moment in her late twenties, when her plane crashed on Christmas Eve, 8,000 feet above sea level in a swamp outside Mexico City.

There were several deaths, but Ina lived to tell a horrific first-person account of the tragedy, although she lost all her hearing for five months. True to her nature she has since reframed the entire experience into a positive one: The plane crash "made me realize that you have to live for today, because this moment is all we have."

She has been diligent and determined about creating a career for herself in a field that is male-dominated. Her work has provided many exceptional experiences, but according to Ina, probably the two greatest highlights were negotiating for the Who, the first rock band to play the Metropolitan Opera House, and negotiating the first international contract to be signed by a Soviet rock star, Boris Grebenshikov. Her time in the Soviet Union, where she collected lacquer boxes and oil paintings, was particularly meaningful, because Russia had been the homeland of her mother and she had always felt a poignant connection even though her mother eagerly left there as a young girl. Ina is proud of her mother who began a career in sculpture ten years ago at the age of sixty-nine. "I hope that in my old age I am as fulfilled as my mother is now. She's very talented."

Even though her life has been filled with exceptionally good fortune (and exceedingly hard work), the break-up in her mid-forties of an eight-year marriage was a traumatic event about which she speaks openly. Few of us know what it's like to be a rock lawyer, but we all know how it feels to have a broken heart.

Finishing up with our interview, Ina invited me to "a real New York experience." We hopped in a taxi and drove to the end of Fifth Avenue in the Village where we settled into a window table at the Rose Café. As comfortable with each other as if we had lived through both the worst and the best parts of our lives together as friends, we carried on our conversation—Ina animated, I somewhat reflective, and, it being February 14th, both of us joking about being each other's "date" for Valentine's Day.

When I graduated from college I wasn't planning to go to law school. I wanted to go to California with my boyfriend. The summer after graduation I studied speedwriting and typing, and elementary education so that I could get a job. My mother's best friend, Ann Mathis, was a lawyer. She was around during my entire childhood. I loved and adored her. I thought she was the most fascinating woman I'd ever met. All that summer she drove me crazy, nagging me about the courses I was taking: "What are you doing with your life? Are you crazy? Is this all you're going to do?"

Actually, what I really wanted to do was join the foreign service, but I wasn't old enough to take the test. Finally, Ann said, "Look, why don't you just take the law boards, and if you don't do well I'll never bother you again." I took the exam with a cavalier attitude—everyone else was scared—and did very well. And that set the course of my life. I have always taken opportunities that have come my way, and I've seized each one and taken full advantage of it.

My next stroke of luck came when I met Morris Ernst. He was a famous lawyer who had been the attorney for the *Ulysses* case and the Margaret Sanger birth control cases, and had also been involved with the Rosenbergs. It was like meeting Oliver Wendell Holmes. He was a crazy character, who took me under his wing and introduced me to copyright law, which I loved. In my last year of law school I was hired by a firm which represented several well-known British music groups. They were good to me and made me a partner when I was only twenty-five. I learned a great deal from those guys, because they just threw me into the work. On my first day I was told to write a contract. I almost dropped dead! I was repeatedly thrown into new situations, and I handled them. This was when I got my first client, the Who; they have been with me the longest. That was the beginning.

The people I've represented have been interesting, because they've turned my head on, and I don't mean just in regards to business. Patti Smith shared aspects of poetry and art with me that I knew nothing about before. Bob Geldof and Pete Townshend each exposed me to a new world. I've watched all my clients grow and develop and change, and I've learned that you can do almost anything you want to do in this world—if you are focused on it. Most people are filled with fear and it's that fear which holds us back.

I've functioned in this business surrounded by all kinds of crazy things that went on, and I never saw or was affected by any of it. Part of me is like Little Mary Sunshine. I was brought up kosher, and I keep a kosher home. In this crazy business, keeping kosher always lets me know who I am. The other reason is my father wouldn't eat in my home if I didn't keep kosher.

My parents have been married for more than fifty years. I consider myself fortunate to have such great parents. I love and adore them, and truly enjoy their company. I have fun with them which I find is very rare. I've met some interesting people through my parents. And they've met my clients. We've been included in each others' lives.

My marriage broke up in my forties. Whether or not someone wants it, a separation is traumatic. It took me quite a while to come back into myself again. So in that sense, part of my forties was very, very tough. I came from a family in which divorce was unheard of—when you got married it was forever. I really believed that. I'm a victim of Doris Day. If I ever write my autobiography it will be called *I Hate You, Doris Day*, because her films taught us that life turns out a certain way but it really doesn't. At the time of my divorce, a close friend told me that "the saddest moment in your life is when you discover that you *don't* die of a broken heart." My work saved me—it was so engaging. It consumed a great deal of time, and time heals many sorrows. Divorce is a major change in your life; it goes to the heart of your being, in terms of how you view things, how things view you. You lose your best friend.

I have to say I probably feel better about myself now than ever before because I didn't break after my divorce. Something happened inside me: I came out the other side of despair. I wake up every morning feeling lucky. I know many working women who don't like their work and are underpaid for what their skills are worth. There's definitely a male club that exists in the record business. Fortunately I've been able to stake out a territory for myself, and be well accepted. I love the fact that I still find things that are challenging, because it's the new work that interests me much more than the old routine. The glamour of the business is what everyone else gets off on, but I've been doing it for so long, it's become less glamorous for me.

I continue to do things I've never done before. I produced a Broadway show about five years ago, a musical of *The Three Musketeers*. I lost a fortune, but I had the greatest time! How many people can say they've produced a Broadway show?

Success means different things at different times in your life. When I was younger, success was about making money, getting well-known in my field, and being well-respected. As you get older, success comes from within; it comes from being happy with yourself and your personal and spiritual evolution, being able to feel that you learned something, did it well, and got pleasure from that.

My fantasy of aging is to age well . . . sort of a combination of Margaret Mead, Georgia O'Keeffe, and Eleanor Roosevelt, with a little Simone Signoret or Simone de Beauvoir thrown in. My dream is to reach a point where age is irrelevant. I want to continue having new experiences. There are many areas of study I want to pursue. I love to travel. I haven't been to Japan, Africa or India yet. I hope to meet someone who's also had a diversity of experiences, and who is ready to play, because I'm ready to play!

I cannot relate to the age I am, because I'm in such a young business. There are many people I represent with whom I feel sympatico, and who are half my age or less. Sometimes I think, "I can't believe I'm twice this person's age, it's impossible!" However, that's the advantage of being in this business: If you're lucky enough to maintain an inner life along with your outer life, it does keep you young.

I feel that there is something new on its way to me, and I want to be available to it. I want to continue to be open to change, which is the hardest thing of all. Change is fearful. I see many people stuck, but I won't let that happen to me.

The one thing I would have done differently is to have had children. I've been divorced about three and a half years, and although I like families, I wouldn't want to be a single parent. It's a hell of a life for a kid. I hope that someday perhaps I'll meet someone who has kids, and they will become my family. But I have to say, despite my disappointments, I have a wonderful and exciting life, with many close friends. When you look back it's easy to say what you might have done, but the reality is, I've had a ball and I expect it to continue. ∎

If a woman doesn't have a sense of herself, now are the years to create it, because you have a backlog of experiences to call upon, patterns that you can see clearly if you are honest with yourself. These coming middle years, as you grow to cronehood, will be the ones that create the cauldron that you will fill in those great final years.

—Elena Featherston

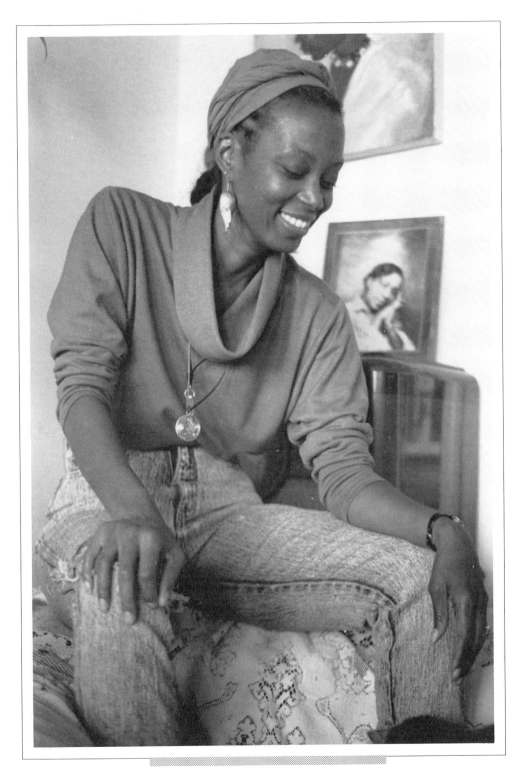

Elena Featherston

To describe Elena Featherston as outspoken is to understate seriously and misrepresent the full range of her character, for she is enormously reflective, of herself and the society in which she lives, and equally honest about both.

I first met Elena at a screening of her first film, *Alice Walker, Visions of the Spirit*. This documentary of the poet, novelist, and essayist received the Black Filmmaker's of America award for Best Documentary Film of 1988. As she now reflects upon her life, she understands that "theatre, or something like it," has always been in her soul. The eye has always been there; but it took years, and "a final discontent" in order to synthesize her talents in the areas of dance, music, theatre, and writing into the medium of film.

Since the time of the civil rights movement, Elena has spent years watching and listening, becoming increasingly cognizant of social situations. She now sees examples of racism continuously. As an illustration of the basic institutionalized concepts of racism in America, Elena alluded to a television commercial for a well-known perfume company in which the evocative voice of Nat King Cole serenades three dancing white women to the refrains of "Unforgettable." "Are they suggesting," Elena rhetorically questioned, "that black men find white women unforgettable? Or that the *only* unforgettable women are white women?" I could not answer her. I became embarrassed by and impatient with my own form of racism: a lack of vigilant and empathic awareness to the pervasiveness of the problem of racism for all people of color.

One day, three years ago, Elena responded deeply, viscerally, to a stereotypic, negative depiction of an African American woman. She was enraged and thought repeatedly, "Why don't they. . .? Why don't they. . .?" Experiencing a sudden epiphany she said to herself, "Why don't YOU?" Elena knew that "they" were not responsible for her vision, and that if she wanted to see accurate depictions of African American women, she must be responsible for creating them. This was the embryonic incident which would eventually lead her to make the award-winning film on Alice Walker.

Elena recalls that there was "a lot of adversity: my brother dying, the dissolution of a relationship, many things." But continuing her work on the film was the connecting thread which kept her going, and sustaining her belief in the project was what kept her "sane."

Elena acknowledges that it was during the making of the documentary that she gave birth to herself. "There was something here I needed to do, something I needed to say. I knew it must be done and said, even if I never did or said anything else." She learned not to be terrorized by the tyranny of expertise, to trust herself, her intuition, her vision.

During our conversation we explored a variety of subjects: women's rights, the plight of the African American woman as artist, her recent abortion, the necessity for creativity in one's life, the replacement of romantic love with "informed" love in her relationships with men, and her sense of "matriarchal responsibility" to protect her son from the "abominations of the U.S. military." During our afternoon dialogue, no topic was too personal or taboo. Elena was free-spirited as well as free-spoken about herself and her life experiences.

ELENA FEATHERSTON

I was born and raised in Richmond, California, a small town that has never been particularly interesting. It was in the middle of nowhere, and had great empty fields of green, growing plants. As a child it provided for me a place to create dreams and a safe haven in which to grow, to be whomever I wanted. This is something my mother also nurtured in me. I had a great deal of fantasy time. One of the most vivid memories that I have—and something that always conjures childhood for me—is hiding in the space between honeysuckle and a fence, smelling the honeysuckle on warm days, reading, and listening to distant airplanes droning overhead. The dreams that I had in that hollow space with that sound and with those books have never, ever gone away. It was a world of infinite possibilites.

A love of travel was born there and a love of books. I read slowly because well-written books create worlds. Sometimes if they were worlds I enjoyed I didn't want to leave them. I began to conjure my own pictures of what the world was about, and fantasized myself into these worlds, creating long and complex dramas in which I'd force my brother and my neighborhood friends to indulge me and to engage in.

The dream to be an actress was born there, the dream to be a dancer, the dreams to do those things that black women normally didn't do. In fact, repeatedly I was told by sensible people that "Blacks don't do that!" So many of the things they said blacks didn't do I did. My mother simultaneously said, "Be practical, be a teacher," and "You can do whatever you want to do." She indulged me with ballet and classical piano lessons. She gave me a sense that there was someone who believed that the things I aspired to had importance, if for no other reason than because I wanted them to feed my spirit. Whether or not the world would accept me as this was irrelevant. What was relevent was my desire. My mother was very supportive, and she worked long, hard hours in order to help me fulfill those dreams.

My mother may not have been a classic feminist, but during a time when most women continued to put up with bad relationships come hell or high water, she chose to leave her marriage and make her own way in the world. She taught me less by what she said than by what she did. She taught me that I had value as a human being and as a woman; that I had a purpose independent of men.

She taught me valuable lessons about what it means to be a parent and the kind of sacrifices that you might have to make for your children. I learned to be intolerant of anyone in my life, particularly men, who would treat me with dishonor or disrespect, or who would behave without integrity and dignity themselves.

At the same time she was able to ground me and impart certain values, some of which I rebelled against. I am grateful for the spirituality my mother imbued in me; she is a deeply spiritual woman. She instilled in me a sense of ritual, the sense of being able to affect your reality. My mother did it with prayer. I may do it differently, but I understand that there is an energy in the universe of which I am a part, and I can affect my life in very real ways. This is empowering. She taught me that I had a right to both conjure and make things manifest. I learned there is a divinity I can speak to, that can affect change in my life—something larger than myself that I can lean against, that will carry me through adversity. All of this I learned from my mother.

My mother was a nurse and worked long hours. I was left to myself a great deal; this was perfect for me. She was over–protective and I needed a lot of space to explore things, so I was blessed when she had to work a bizarre shift, the evening three-to-eleven shift. It was wonderful because it meant that most days when I came home from school my mother was gone and wouldn't return until 11:30 at night. I could do anything I damn well pleased as long as I kept up appearances, and my being a hellion just wasn't too, too obvious. It gave me extraordinary freedom.

The years between eleven and fourteen were rich for me. They were the years during which I had my greatest insights, when my true self was the strongest and held sway. When I talk about being my best self, I think I am really talking about manifesting as an adult the realities that I sensed in those three years. During that time I was definitely different and alien. I was inside myself and felt alone but not disconnected. I learned of my connection to the earth, to all living beings, to all living things. Most of those lessons I've tried to honor, because they were other-worldly for me. I felt that I was receiving valuable information. To the best of my ability I've tried to stay on the path, because there was a truth in my youthful intuition, there was truth in my insights.

I made up my mind by the time I was twelve that I would never marry. Marriage is a very lopsided contract. If I could understand that at twelve, why should I be an idiot in my twenties or thirties and convince myself that somehow it had changed? It still hasn't. Marriage carries many assumptions. As part of this culture, I carry them, but they are still unhealthy. Rather than placing myself in an unhealthy situation, I would rather work consciously on each relationship day-to-day and make them the best that I possibly can for as long as they last.

I didn't marry the father of my children. We were "in love" and we lived together, and we both thought that marriage was stupid, so we never bothered. As I pointed out to my mother, marriage is not a biological process. Having children is, and I didn't need to get married in order to do this. People have a tendency to invest in the illusion of another person. That's what I call romantic love. I'm not interested in romantic love any more; I want informed love. I want to know who you are, to be your ally and friend; I want to know that some things you do put a boil on my butt, and that I will be able to deal with them. And *then* I want to love you.

I don't know if I want to live in the same space with another person. Again, that may be part of the romantic illusion about what love and life and men and women are about. Part of the patriarchal love model has to do with the feminine woman and the perfect man who come together and make each other whole. No! No! No! It should be a choice to live with someone because it works for you both. People tend to think that the level of commitment to the relationship is less if they don't live together. But instead there is a great deal of freedom and fluidity and flexibility. The relationship is no longer taken for granted.

For instance, last night I sat in my office and filed papers until late. That's what I needed to get done, and I wouldn't have wanted to stop at eight because my partner had come home and wanted my attention. I started at three and worked until midnight; that was my flow. We don't pay attention to these things; we tend to be neglectful of our own rhythms. We need to rethink relationships from the top down. The whole concept of love is based on the romantic model. And it appeals to us because we have heard those fairy tales since we were pre-verbal.

I will beat the person who tells my granddaughter about Snow White, or Cinderella, or any of those other women who waited for some prince to come along and solve their problems. The end of the story is always, "...they lived happily ever after." No one ever tells you what struggles they had to endure in order to do that. You just somehow get flipped off your feet by some prince, and then everything is fine forever.

While the conscious mind is saying, "Of course this is not true," subconsciously, this insidious shit has worked on you without you knowing it. You expect the other person to be everything, and then you both begin to lose yourselves in one another, ultimately resenting that loss of self and expecting the other to compensate. The more you do that, the more you dig yourself into an emotional hole, an emotional rut, destroying any possibility for a real relationship.

I don't think I will ever live with a lover again on an ongoing basis. But, if I do, he will have a place of his own to go when we're working on each other's nerves. That's important. Maybe that bonding with the father is needed when you are raising a child. But I don't need it now. I'm forty-three years old and I've raised my children.

Recently I had an incredible experience. I never believed the biological clock story—certainly not for a woman who had raised two children! But a year ago I got pregnant. Some close friends of mine had a baby, and another set of friends had adopted a child. When I held one of them in my arms, I said, "Oh God, I would love to have a child." This was foolish for a woman who understands the power of words. Two months later I discovered I was pregnant. In some ways it was magnificent, but I realized that Paul and I did not want to have a baby. We have *adult* children. I'm a grandmother! Am I out of my mind?! I went through that process very intensely—wanting the child, not wanting the child—finally making the decision to have an abortion, and going through with it.

I had a dreadful sense of having taken something away from myself. I'm not one of those people who deals in what I consider euphemism. I mean, if pro-life advocates want to say to me, "Do you understand that you are commiting a murder?" I would answer, "Yes." The choice is to kill a fetus or destroy a child emotionally. I was thinking first and foremost of the child. It is a murder of a different sort, a more insidious one, not to be there in the way that a child needs. It would also have destroyed me at this stage of my life. That was not the way I was meant to manifest my creativity. I was supposed to be creating something else. There would have been two deaths, three, possibly four, because I wouldn't be there for Alex in a grandmother mode while in a mother mode. I would not want to be walking those two paths at the same time.

This is something that we need to recognize and talk about. I'm not advocating abortion. If a woman is pregnant and she wants to keep the baby, Elena says do it. But it wasn't the thing I should be doing, it wasn't the thing Paul should be doing. There were several lives to consider, including the life of the child. I had been blessed with the gift which I had so thoughtlessly asked for. I was careless. It was probably singularly the most difficult thing I have ever had to do, to bond and to say good-bye. Perhaps if my daughter chooses to have another child that spirit will come back into my life in a way that I can give it what it truly needs—as a grandmother, not as a mother.

Women should talk about these things. During a time of threatened oppression of women's rights, I wondered how I could ever have been so lax as to take the right to abortion for granted. It became apparent to me what they are trying to steal from my daughter and my granddaughter. It's just not right.

I am forty-three and I accept being middle-aged. I'm watching my body change, but my veneration for ancestors and age hold me in good stead. I look at my body and think, "Wow! I don't have a body like a

fourteen-year-old boy any more! I have hips! This is a woman's body."
I feel good about that. The flip side of that is that it's all well and
good to grow older, but I want my body to be strong and firm, to be the
best body it can be. And then gravity and time can do whatever they are
going to do. Aging is inevitable. How I'm going to do it is a toss-up. At
the moment, I feel good about it. I was not big on exercising before,
so why am I so big on it now? Because my butt is headed south, that's
why!

An example of my fantasy of aging is Ruth Gordon, who main-
tained an extraordinary sense of the child in herself. I want to have that
sense of the dream, and the vision that there is always something just
around the corner that remains for me to do.

The other fantasy, the ultimate fantasy, of aging is Lena Horne,
which is—never to do it—to just grow older and become increasingly
more exquisite, to become an ageless goddess! When I think of aging, I
see it in magical terms, as a tension in myself between nymph and crone.
At some point in time, that tension breaks, and all of the physical
attributes I see as youth, and many of the things that I've used to carry
me through life, will suddenly change. And if I have lived well, lived
with wisdom, in that hollow place that is created by the break will be all
of these new ways of being. They will make themselves manifest, and I
will have the time to become the human being who I am supposed to be
so that, when I finally die, it will be with ease, and with peace. My
intent is to grow richer and richer until the body winds down and stops.
I want to remain feisty and sexy straight up until the very last. Yes! Yes!
Yes! I want that last orgasm three days before I go to the other side.

I'm not happy unless I'm thinking about, planning, or working on a
project. And my projects are always subversive. By subversive I mean

taking a look at the myths, traditions, and ideas that constitute what is normal in our culture, and questioning it, looking at it differently; being brave enough to be the little boy who says, "But the emperor isn't wearing any clothes." Once you can see that the emperor is naked, once you can see the foundations of what's driving your life—driving *you*, not just the culture—are not what they appear to be, you are never the same again.

The idea that there is *one* culture, *one* reality—that things can be put neatly into one little box which works for everyone—simply is not true. That way of thinking is crippling and it's almost a criminal thing to do to the human spirit. My way of subverting this is to say, "I won't let you do it to me. This is my life, and I intend to live it just my way." In doing that I don't intend to hurt or offend anyone unnecessarily, but I won't hurt and offend my spirit in order to live life in a way that makes you comfortable." My experience must be real, it must be authentic, it must derive from my true self, not the self that other people try to invent for me. That, to me, is the ultimate in creativity. How creativity is expressed is irrelevant. I don't care if it's collage, or painting, or really good banana bread. As long as it's being expressed.

My next documentary project is an eight-part series called *We Were Not Meant to Survive*. It is a thematic look at African American women writers in America from 1746 to the present. It looks at those themes through three lenses: the suspended, the assimilated, and the emergent.

I think of the women in slavery through the 1860s in this country as being suspended. The forces in their lives were so intense that they had few options about what to do and where to go. They were held suspended by circumstances. And many of the women were broken by those circumstances, but not in spirit. Obviously they were survivors. I look back at them and I know if they could survive that, I can survive anything and thrive.

The next group of women were the assimilated, the women from the 1900s through the 1950s, who tried to assimilate into the white culture. These women judged themselves as the culture judged them, not by what they were, but by what they weren't. They weren't white, blond, petite, or frail. African American women got into aspiring to be what was defined as the "real woman" by white standards. It wasn't only African American women—poor white women also were striving to be the "real woman."

An emergent woman of the post-civil rights movement, post '60s, '70s says, "Excuse me, I am an African American. My hair is nappy sometimes, my skin is dark, I am not white, these are my roots, this is how my body moves, my butt is big, my mouth is bigger, my attitude is worse and if you get in my face I will kick yo' ass! These are my terms for humanity. Accept it or get out of my face, because this is who I intend to be." And being perfectly happy with that. You see that in the writings of Alice Walker and Toni Morrison. The themes that these women write about are repeated over and over again in African American women's literature.

So many women became self-destructive, committed suicide, or went crazy because of racism. I think increasing numbers of African American women of all ages in this decade are saying, "We are not going to commit suicide, we are not going to go crazy, and we are not going to tell the stories and paint the pictures that you want to hear and see. We are going to tell *our* stories and paint *our* pictures." It is difficult because, if you do that, few people want to publish or exhibit your work. No one wants to acknowledge it. There is still the effort to silence.

A different kind of black woman is emerging at this time. We are still resilient. We still survive. The anger of women of color will be an invaluable coinage—more valuable than gold, because it is a thing of the spirit. For people of color, art, for a long time, has been a tool of protest. That's what gospel songs and blues songs and work songs were about.

It is the work of people who are oppressed, dealing with oppression—saying things they need to say, between the lines, and painting pictures they need to paint, between the brushstrokes. That's what art has been for many people of color, all over the world, for a very, very long time.

I do my best work when I get angry. My friends tease me, "If you want Elena to get articulate, piss her off." No wonder people don't want you to get angry, you become precise, you become focused, you become empowered. That makes a lot of people uncomfortable. I don't believe I should value their comfort over my truth. Not *the* truth, *my* truth. I think of creativity as a reason not to be destructive, though much of my creativity ultimately comes out of my anger. Anger is an incredibly valuable thing to women of color because it is the thing that we are denied. If we speak out and speak with passion, we are considered angry. Our anger is treated as somehow debasing to us. Not so.

After I started filmmaking, I realized that I had been in training to be a filmmaker all of my life. You need ritual, you need to work collaboratively, you need to be a storyteller, to have the eye of the subject, and you need to get inside of someone else and have a transformative experience in order to do those things. I can see things now from both sides of the camera—I know how a director thinks from all my years of theatre, how an actress thinks from all my years of acting. I understand composition; I also know how to do things collaboratively and creatively so that I allow people's talents to flow. I think this is what I've been working towards; this is the fantasy life I created for myself when I was a child—the kind of world that I wanted to live in and work in. The most I can say about creativity is that it keeps reintroducing me to myself on a deeper and deeper level. The deeper I go, the more I learn, the more I have to say, and the more I can hear what someone else has to say.

When I discovered filmmaking, I discovered the thing that makes me happy. The only thing that makes me happier is writing, and I see them as being similar. All of the creative forms are important to me, because they are ways of getting the best of what's inside me out and sharing it with others, being able to dialogue with others.

If I make a film, or write a piece, then I am sharing a subversive thought with others. At that point I have had a dialogue with many other people, some of whom I will never physically meet, and some whom, mercifully, I will. With those I meet there will be a further dialogue and we will have a place from which to build. I think that's so important in our world.

The only advice I have for other women approaching forty, or who are in their forties, is to, "Sit back, girl, and enjoy it. The worst is over; the best is yet to come. You have survived. You have met adversity, made decisions, and solved problems. You have done stupid things and cried your tears, but you have survived! You can create beauty in your life. You have had forty years of experience, so you can live the next forty or fifty years informed."

If a woman doesn't have a sense of herself, now are the years to create it, because you have a backlog of experiences to call upon, patterns that you can see clearly if you are honest with yourself at this juncture in your life. These coming middle years, as you grow to cronehood, will be the ones that create the cauldron that you will fill in those great final years. ■

What is it that sustains me through the difficult periods? It is the experience [of writing]. Sure, there is satisfaction with people saying to you, I love your work. That's fine, but believe me, if you are dependent on that for your satisfaction, you are up a creek . . . you begin to learn that when you are in your forties.

—Susan Griffin

Susan Griffin

We are the bird's eggs. Bird's eggs, flowers, butterflies, rabbits, cows, sheep; we are caterpillars; we are leaves of ivy and sprigs of wallflower. We are women. We rise from the wave. We are gazelle and doe, elephant and whale, lilies and roses and peach, we are air, we are flame, we are oyster and pearl, we are girls. We are women and nature.

—Susan Griffin, *Woman and Nature*

In the late 1970s I was given and subsequently read a book which utterly articulated and affirmed a silent knowing deep within me which I had carried since I was a young girl: that I was inextricably and inevitably connected to nature. And that the blood which coursed through my veins was indeed like the rivers flowing across the body of the earth. The book was *Woman and Nature: The Roaring Inside Her*, by Susan Griffin.

I was stunned by the beauty of its poetic and unconventional blending of philosophy, history, and political theory. It consequently altered my perception of what it means to be female in Western culture and awakened not only the ideology of but the visceral necessity for feminism in my life.

I have remained in awe of the intellectual capacity which is evident in Susan Griffin's successive writings, *Pornography and Silence, Rape: The Politics of the Unconscious, Made from this Earth*, and several collections of poetry, the most recent being *Unremembered Country*. But in truth it has been the coupling of the scholarly approach with a deep emotional rendering that has made her writing most profound for me: how Griffin's writing conveys the way in which a woman feels through the womb, before perceiving with the mind.

In her current book, *The Chorus of Stones: The Private Life of War*, Griffin investigates the ways in which our private lives have been affected by—and have affected—war; how the personal and the public are inseparable. Her analysis springs from a deep intuitive sense as well as research.

For six years Susan Griffin has been struggling with Chronic Fatigue Syndrome (CFIDS), an illness that attacks the immune system, which is also known as Epstein-Barr. Our conversation was sobering, because it primarily dealt with the most fragile of human fears: debilitating sickness and death. Due to her personal experience, she has sought to understand why, in the last half of the 20th century there is a catastrophic break-down in the human immune system, indicating the influence of a polluted environment on its inhabitants, and what can be done about it.

SUSAN GRIFFIN

There are things I would have done differently in my life. Definitely. I would have been much more health-conscious from an earlier age. I happen to have been born with a body that's not very strong, and I now have a fairly serious illness, chronic fatigue immune dysfunctional syndrome. I don't know how long I've had this but I think it's about six years. I'm feeling that we all should do as much as we can to build up our health. Unfortunately, I think this is an unnatural situation that's been created by the degree of pollution.

I was born in Los Angeles in the '40s and grew up in the '50s. Like everyone else I was exposed to low-level radiation during my growing years from the atmospheric testing in Nevada and New Mexico. Then this was combined with an unprecedented amount of pollution in food. My mother did and still does use a lot of processed foods. She was in the generation that thought this was miraculous. In a way it was substituted for a liberation from the female role that needed to take place, not technologically but politically. If you look at it historically, you see that women in the '20s had a burst into freedom that got lost in the '30s. Then with the war, women again experienced some freedom, but that was entirely lost in the '50s, which was when I grew up. There was an onslaught of media advice from every corner saying, "go back to the home, give up your jobs, let men have the jobs, raise your children." It's what Betty Friedan wrote about in the *Feminine Mystique* which was really the first widely read modern feminist text published in America, outside of the translation of Simone de Beauvoir's *The Second Sex*. And so, I grew up in that period of the '50s and my mother was also molded by that. She was always the one who stayed at home, even though she was very interested in interior decoration and studied it for a while.

She was very intelligent. But everyone was saying, "What you need to do is stay at home and raise your children." She became an alcoholic.

I think the fact that she was deprived of any significance in her life, other than the traditional female role, certainly played a part in that alcoholism. In our early understanding of alcoholism Jung made the connection with Spirit, that the word is the same for alcohol and Spirit. In the life of the alcoholic, there is a killing of the Spirit. That is what happens to a woman who is literally denied the right to develop her capacities, her soul capacities, which are tied to the capacities to create.

In a way women were bought off with these technological advances. When we think of the '50s we think of Betty Furness standing by her electric refrigerator, or Ronald Reagan saying, "Progress is our most important product." The decade of the '50s was a period of spiritual degeneration, or, certainly, stagnation, and not only for women. People really couldn't quite face the horrors of the Holocaust and of Hiroshima. They couldn't face the horrors that had happened in the world during the course of the two world wars, and so there was a general retraction into a traditional way of life that had become hollow. What we ended up with was a kind of deadness. People need something enlivening, and what replaced it all was technology. When people looked for excitement in their lives, men or women, there was no content to it. There was not any sort of spiritual quest any longer. There wasn't even any physical bravery.

A whole generation of us grew up in this super-technological age. We now use an enormous amount of electricity and eat food which is filled with every sort of chemical substance. No one really knows what the cumulative effect of all these things is.

There isn't anybody in responsible positions at this point in world health organizations who is saying, "Let's really reevaluate this and take a sober look at it. We're not talking about throwing the baby out with the bathwater, but let's look at the combined effect of all these things."

It's astonishing that no one has, really.

And now what I see around me are many people in our forties and fifties with our health breaking down in a way that didn't happen before. It used to be that if you made it to thirty or forty, then you would live until seventy or eighty, unless something catastrophic happened. And yes, there were a few people who got cancer or something serious, but it was really a minority. It wasn't every third person, the way it is now, battling with something that is either life-threatening or completely disabling.

How could I have known then? I suppose that one of my purposes is to communicate to younger people how critical ecological issues are. Those of us who are ill ought to be seen as "the canaries in the coal mine." Of course the reality is even deeper. If one among us is ill, we are all ill. Because we are one. This is self-evident ecologically. But it is also true on every other level. When one person in a society is ill, the whole social body is ill, and one has to look to the social body both for the cause and the cure of the disease. For instance a certain kind of technology can produce a pollution which causes an illness. But what did the technology arise from in the first place? A kind of emptiness perhaps within society. A failure of spirit. So, in order to get well I may have to learn something. But it is not an individual lesson I am learning, nor is it an individual error I am discovering, so much as a shared solution for a social problem. A fate we all share.

I went through a severe attack, and there was no guarantee that I'd come out of it at all. I felt at times close to death, and that it would be better to die than to stay alive like that. It lasted for months and months. It's the hardest thing I've ever been through.

There are other things in my life that were more tragic, more painful, but that was hardest because it went on for months and months.

At the same time, this disease takes away all one's ability to fight, because one is so terribly debilitated and in pain most of the time.

Having the illness forced me to develop a quietness at the core I did not know possible. The harshness of the illness called this up in me. But this quietness I feel can be helpful now in the largest context. To understand one's life in the largest context is in itself healing. To come at this from another door, the experience of illness is itself an antidote to the social ills which caused the illness. This is so whether or not the person who is stricken with illness is part of the social problem. The consequences of history are not spread evenly or justly. But every experience can be transformed into some kind of wisdom, ideally. Not by transcending the experience but by embracing it, by really knowing it.

One of the things that I've learned from the illness is how much there is for us to learn in direct experience. The knowledge we have come to value most highly in this society is that which we can measure scientifically. But experience is filled with another kind of knowledge, and in itself will move you toward transformation, because that's the nature of reality.

In your forties you suddenly see yourself as part of the older generation. Not just with regard to children, but to young adults. You do not have to be ill to learn. I have a daughter who is twenty-one and I learn a lot from her. I find that because of my relationship with her, I think often of people that age and the implications of things for them. There are many times that I'm not aware of what she knows. I really do think that when you are older you tend, particularly if you're intellectual and have been relatively successful, to be a little arrogant and think that you know everything. Then you find out that you could very easily be in the category of an old fuddy-duddy, one of these cranky older people who refuses to realize that things have changed and they haven't kept abreast of the world.

It's the question of objectivity. You don't know everything. You only know your slice. At the same time you do know something from having lived this many years, and you have some wisdom to impart. So it's a delicate thing. I find myself in the position with many younger people of being a teacher. For one thing, I've written now for over thirty years and I'm like a master craftsman who really knows how to make a bench. I know—my hands know—things about the structure of a sentence, about the structure of a book. Yet, at the same time, every book I write is something new to me, presents unknown territory, and makes me feel like I'm learning all over again.

I have some very specific knowledge to impart about certain ways of living. And I find that I have become, at the same time, much stronger and much more vulnerable. In this culture we're so used to thinking of vulnerability as being weak. We use this word "wimp," and we think of vulnerability as being soft, feminine. We do not understand that like the experience of illness, vulnerability is a source of enormous wisdom, if it's not separated off from the rest of human qualities, and if it's valued. This is the human condition. In a way when you are younger you can pretend that you're not vulnerable. But at a certain age you don't have the energy to pretend any more. And, paradoxically, there is a certain strength in this, because one has faced one's fears directly.

I don't agree with New Age people who say things always work out. They don't always work out. I mean certainly things did not work out for babies who got napalmed in Viet Nam. It did not work out for a Vietnam vet who's had a schizophrenic breakdown and been hospitalized for ten years. That's not working out.

But the truth is that you're lucky, when a terrible situation comes

64

along, if you are able to make something good out of it, like the Vietnamese made friendship rings from the parts of airplanes that fell over their land. I always remember that from the period when we were trying to stop that war. It always moved me.

I feel that if I had had this illness at an earlier age, I'm not sure my psyche would have survived it with the same kind of strength that I've survived it now. I think it's good luck that I am that much stronger now, because it was a horrific experience.

It's difficult to get at what I mean about vulnerability and strength. It's one of those things that is so self-evident if you have lived through it; and yet it runs so against the grain of this culture that it's hard to explain. This is a metaphor that's working for me right now because of the 1989 earthquake. I recently had foundation work done on my house. A house with a weak foundation can't sustain various kinds of shocks. So it's better to have a strong foundation. Now, if you are out of touch with your vulnerability, you are building a big superstructure over a very tiny foundation. It's an inflation, it's brittle, because it's not connected to the depth. But if you are connected to your feelings of loss and sadness—what some people call "the dark," the realm of the psyche that's not socially accepted, that's hidden—if you know that, then you are connected all the way down to the ground. You have a firm foundation. You're of a piece. And when something comes along that's difficult to deal with, you are a flexible structure. You are not going to break because you're connected all the way through.

My oldest practice has been my work, my writing; as far back as I can remember, I have treated it as a practice. I have ambition like anybody else, but I never wanted simply money and fame. I wanted to experience myself through the writing, experience a kind of depth. And very early on I realized that experiencing myself through the writing was as important as anything I produced.

And I had to attend to the way I was during the writing, that it wasn't enough just to put words on paper, but that my state of mind was extremely important. (And I teach this with my students.)

What you need to attend to is your state of mind while you're working. If you are feeling alienated from the process, you're not going to be able to create anything but alienation for the reader. Whatever you are doing to yourself, the work is going to do to the reader. I'm at the stage in my writing where I can turn anything into elegant prose, but it won't necessarily have any spirit. I can even create a sort of false spirit, but I know the difference, and it gives me a sort of sick feeling if it's fake.

For instance, I just finished a section on Gandhi in my book *The Chorus of Stones: The Private Life of War*. In its first draft, it told a story about Gandhi, but it was merely description; there was something missing. It just didn't have a heart to it. I realized I had to drop down into Gandhi's experience; I had to go into myself and find the place inside where I understood what Gandhi was talking about when he fasted, and that was amazing. Right now I'm just in love with Gandhi. I feel that he is my teacher. He became my teacher because I actually went inside his consciousness—insofar as one can do that imaginatively. In my process, I'll write something, I'll go to sleep, I'll have a feeling of uneasiness about it, and I'll know I have to go further with it. It's a constant dialogue with myself, and I'm not willing to buy myself off easily.

I guess what I'm talking about is a process that demands integrity. Many people think that it's virtuous, that the person is being good, but it has nothing to do with that. If I were just trying to be good, it would be boring, I think. It's what Gandhi was talking about with fasting. If you are attached to the outcome, you lose the inner joy. For me it's this joy in the process of writing, this joy of discovery, that has kept me going. I've been working on this book for six years. The material has at times been absolutely harrowing just to listen to and take in. It has affected my dreams.

I've had CFIDS for six years, even though part of that time it wasn't diagnosed. I've had to work triple-schedule sometimes just to make ends meet. Right now I'm totally broke. I may have to mortgage my house to be able to write the end of the book. Why would anyone continue with something like this? Although you might write a book that will produce a lot of good effects at the end, that will bring you personal pleasures like good reviews, or money, or God knows what, that's not enough to sustain you unless you're crazy. But when I push the book to where *it* needs to go, I get such incredible joy I can't tell you. There's nothing like it. It's the most wonderful feeling. It's like being in love but having a relationship with the whole world; it's exquisite. That is what sustains me through the difficult periods—the experience. Sure, there is satisfaction with people saying to you, I love your work. That's fine, but, believe me, if you're dependent on that for your satisfaction, you are up a creek. I think that is something you begin to learn when you are in your forties. So this joy is what keeps me honest and gives me steady sustenance. ■

Forty was the beginning of putting together the skills that I had acquired through my personal life, my education, and my work experience. Turning forty was great; it was the decade that I gave myself to public service.

—Barbara Boxer

Barbara Boxer

▪ P R O F I L E ▪

I heard her before I saw her. I was scheduled to meet with Congresswoman Barbara Boxer early on a Friday morning at her "Boxer for Senate" campaign headquarters situated a half-block away from San Francisco City Hall. Waiting in the ballroom-sized front office where I watched her campaign manager, Ed McGovern, brainstorm with the mostly volunteer crew, a burst of throaty laughter reverberated out in the hall. "That's Barbara!" smiled Ed. Barbara, short even in heels, was wearing an attractive magenta and black dress, and I couldn't help imagining her sitting among hundreds of monotonous gray or blue suits in the House of Representatives, and thinking how striking she must appear in those surroundings. After offering me coffee and a bite of her zucchini muffin, we settled into our interview.

Barbara Boxer answered the questions succinctly and politely, the politician in her ever-present. She represents Marin County and portions of San Francisco. She uses her brand of dynamic leadership to preserve the environment, mobilize against AIDS, protect women's rights, reform military procurement, and defend basic freedoms for all Americans. She is an articulate feminist who has been on the leading edge of progressive change throughout her political career.

Married for nearly thirty years, with two adult children who have now become her "friends and supporters," her political life started by organizing anti-war rallies in her back yard in 1967 when her son, Doug, was two, her daughter, Nicole, was four months old, and the Vietnam War had become a concern to millions of Americans. Deeply affected by the assassinations of both Martin Luther King and Robert Kennedy, Barbara felt she would "go crazy," if she didn't do something, take action of some kind.

And do something she has. Barbara Boxer is increasingly viewed as a national leader for the Pro-Choice Movement and, like many supporters of a woman's right to have a safe, legal abortion, Boxer has indicated the need to reduce the number of abortions through better contraception and improved dispersion of family planning information. She is also a longtime advocate for numerous energy conservation measures including reducing our dependence on fossil fuels through such means as improved mass transit systems, proper weatherization of homes and public buildings, and increased appliance efficiency.

70

In response to her tireless efforts, Barbara has been honored by such groups as Planned Parenthood, the Center for Environmental Education, the Consumer Federation of America, the Coalition to Stop Government Waste, the League of Conservation Voters, the Humane Society of America, the American Association of University Women, and the Anti-Defamation League, which, during its presentation to her, said:

> If politics is truly the art of the possible, Boxer is a virtuoso of getting things done in Washington.

Imagine a politician who is for all the *right* causes. It may seem like an impossible dream. But Barbara Boxer is alive and well in California, and running for the United States Senate. In her declaration for the candidacy for the 1992 Senate race, she declared: "The people of this state need a fighter to be very outspoken and stand up against the special interests." Her commendable goal in this campaign is nothing short of changing "the face of politics in California." Good luck, Barbara.

BARBARA BOXER

I was a stockbroker with no intention of ever entering politics. My life turned around in the '60s after Martin Luther King and Robert Kennedy were killed, and the Vietnam War broke out. At that time I had two small children and I thought, what kind of world is this? Will they grow up and go to war? Will they live in a world of violence and assassinations? So I got involved. I felt I would literally go crazy if I didn't do something. I had to take action. I've never been the type of person who sits back and complains about something. I have to fix it. My involvement wasn't selfless. In a way it was a selfish thing, because I thought I couldn't survive otherwise.

I wanted to do something in my own community to bring people together. So I started a group of women in the suburbs to help young people who were dropping out of school get jobs or stay in school. We put together a terrific project with a completely volunteer group teaching them receptionist work, telephone answering, general office skills. The project was so good it was eventually taken over by the county schools office.

By 1970 the Vietnam War was raging, and I became involved in the peace movement in Marin. We put a measure on the ballot to end the war. It said, "We call on the president to end the war in Vietnam." People said it would never pass, because Marin County was then a Republican county. But it did pass and that launched me into politics.

In 1972 I first ran for public office, a position on the Board of Supervisors, and lost in a very close race. After that I became a newspaper reporter, doing in-depth stories on everything from the war in Vietnam to politics, the judiciary system, waste problems—any feature story I wanted to write. I won some awards for my writing; I loved it.

When John Burton announced he would run in a special election for Congress, he asked me to organize his campaign in Marin. I left journalism and went to work for John, and, after he won, I worked for him in Congress.

In 1976 I again ran for the Board of Supervisors. This time I won. I was reelected four years later and two years after that when John announced he wouldn't run for Congress again, I ran for his seat. It was a tough, tough race, but I was elected!

Early in my career, being a woman was a disadvantage. I'm convinced that I lost my first race because of sexism. However, now I feel it's an advantage, because people are tired of business as usual—a guy in a suit running for political office. That doesn't mean that every woman has a better chance of being elected than every man—it does mean that people are willing to give a chance to a woman who has proven herself in politics. People are tired of the way things are going; they feel alienated and apathetic. They say, "Well, here's someone who's a little different. Let's see if she will really stand up and be counted."

When I started in politics I was a trailblazer. I didn't realize it at the time. When I first ran for public office, there were eleven women in city councils in Marin. Four years later when I ran again there were fifty-five women. It was clear that, even though I had lost my race, I had given many women the impetus to say, "Well she stuck her neck out, and even if she lost she still has her dignity; she made some changes, she's still alive, she hasn't run away from home. I can do it too!"

We have a golden moment in history right now. The Soviet Union and the United States have resolved the Cold War. That's an enormous step forward. I can see a world in which we develop new ways to resolve crisis, using multinational forums to resolve problems in a peaceful way through economic sanctions and arms agreements.

I'm hopeful that the ingredients are there for a much better future. On the other hand, if the wrong people are in power, we could find ourselves using the same old ways to resolve conflict through violence and war. That's why I'm running for the Senate, because I will speak out for a new foreign policy and a new future where we can begin to pay attention to the crying needs that we have in our own country, rather than continuing to support an enormous military budget to protect everybody else in the world.

I am willing to take on the establishment. I'm not someone who walks in and compromises early on. I say, "Look, this is wrong, and I want to tell you why," and I don't back off. There is plenty of time for backing off, there are plenty of people who will compromise early, but I think we need politicians in the House and Senate who stake out the position that is the right one, and then compromise from there.

Many of my skills began to develop in my thirties. At forty I began to put together the skills that I had acquired through my personal life, my education, and my work experience. Turning forty was great, it was the decade that I gave myself to public service. My life has been enormously rewarding and challenging. I did it all. What I learned is that it is possible simultaneously to have fulfilled personal and work lives. It's challenging, but it's also wonderful. I had to be healthy and energetic. Having the support of my family was crucial to sustaining my political life. Family life keeps reminding me what is important, what is real, as opposed to the political world, which is a harsh environment. You need strength to stand up when people who don't even know you are calling you every name in the book. In my forties I learned that my personal life sustains me in my political life.

Being a mother is one of the best and also one of the hardest things I've ever done. Certainly it is one of the most rewarding. I'm happy I had my children when I was young, because now that my kids are in their twenties, they have become my friends and supporters. When I think of the people I most enjoy being with, they're right on the list. I'm fortunate that my life has worked out this way.

Of course we still experienced the terrible two's and the terrible teens. We went through it all, but we had the knowledge and the trust that we could work through any problems, and we always knew we loved each other. I've been commuting to Washington since my kids were teenagers, and I have hilarious stories about raising my children from the nation's capitol. One morning, about eleven a.m., I was in the middle of questioning Cap Weinberger about the defense budget and was just making my point when my secretary told me my husband was on the phone. I finished the question and answered the phone. There were my husband and daughter both on the line complaining about each other. I just started laughing. What could I do? I was three thousand miles away trying to make peace between them. A telephone is an important tool in my life. AT&T played a major role in bringing up my children.

I don't believe that being away from home has helped or hindered my relationship with my husband. Either a relationship works or it doesn't. But it is difficult to maintain a long-distance relationship unless there is complete knowledge of the person. The fact that we've been married such a long time has made it possible. We've made the most of it and had a lot of fun in the process. Often my husband comes to Washington, and whenever I travel anywhere he comes with me. Now, during the Senate campaign, he travels with me on weekends. During my nine years in Congress, there have been only two weekends when we weren't together. The weekends are our time.

I was thirty-seven when my father died. When you are close to forty years old, you start dealing with your own mortality. So my father died smack in the middle of that period of my life, and it was difficult. I don't look at aging as different from anything else that happens in life. I think you're the same person you've always been, obviously, except you've been around longer and you should be better for it. Your energy level and your appearance may change for the worse, perhaps, your health will suffer. These are the things everyone worries about. The thing to do is to try to stay healthy and in shape and continue to work.

No one lives forever; we're all going to die. The key is to make the most of what you've got every day. I don't worry about it much now. I did when my kids were young, because I knew they needed me. After my mother became ill and before she died, I dealt with the sadness of her death and the fact that she did not die with dignity because she was ill, physically and mentally. That's not the way that I want to leave. That's why my fantasy of getting older is to be healthy and working and active, because I've seen how terrible it is when it's the other way.

I've come to grips with what would happen if I died tomorrow. That's important to do every once in a while, because then you can deal with the things that are unfinished in your life. First and foremost, I want to leave my family a lasting, unconditional love. Unconditional love sustains you through your life whether your parent is there or not, assuming you've had enough time to receive that love; and I think my children have.

In my political life I would like to leave behind a sense that I never was afraid to say what I thought, or to stick my neck out and stand up for what I thought was right or was in the public interest. I have to continue to do what I do and feel proud of it. If I lost my compass, I wouldn't be leaving anything behind, really.

The most satisfying aspect of political life is articulating my constituents' hopes and dreams, and seeing that I can make a connection with people and speak for those who can't really speak for themselves:

powerless children, the disabled, people who care but simply aren't in an arena where they can make a difference.

I feel I've stood tall for protecting the environment, for peace, for choice. I've been willing to debate these issues with the toughest opponents from Pat Buchanan to George Bush. I keep working to prevent myself from getting complacent, or playing safe politics. I'd rather not do politics if I had to do it that way. I will continue to try to articulate issues for people and put ideas forward, trying to move America in what I consider to be a better direction, so that people in this country are fulfilled and they can live up to their potential in peace and prosperity. These are far-reaching goals, but I think in whatever field we're in, we can all do that in our own lives: keep trying to push the country forward.

Success is different for everybody. If everyone's definition of success were the same, it would be boring because we'd all be doing the same thing. To me, success means a balance between my personal life and my work life—they both give me sustenance. Success means that in my personal life, love dominates. In my work life I know I'm making a difference to people, by helping them feel good about themselves, restoring their faith in the process. I help them also by articulating what they want. I would like to go to the United States Senate. If I don't make it, I see myself in various ways continuing to fight for the issues I believe in, with the skills that I have.

One of the best compliments I've had was from a real pro politician who came up to me one day after I'd made a speech on the House floor. He told me, "You say the things so many of us think but somehow never say." That was an incredible compliment. Maybe this ability is a gift. If it is a gift I'm going to use it as best I can. ■

My current view of the world is that life is braided streams of light and darkness, joy and pain, and I just accept them. They both exist and I walk them both. But now I know there is choice about what I do with them. This awareness is one of the delights of being forty.

—Arisika Razak

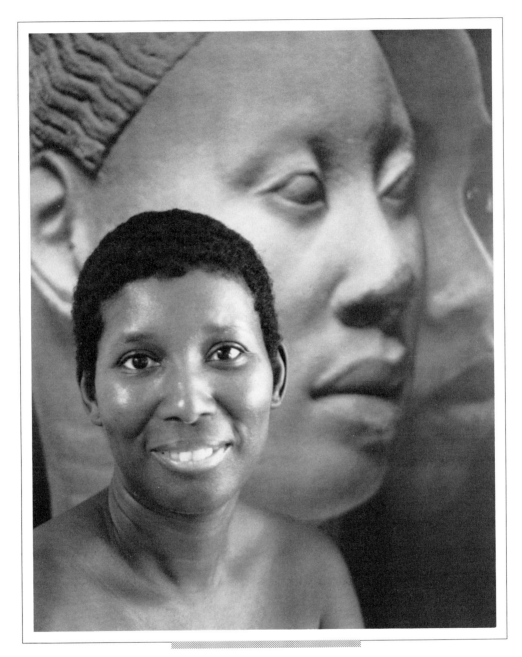

Arisika Razak

In September, 1987 I attended a women's autumn equinox celebration in Northern California. One of the classes available was on African dance. The focus wasn't upon the wild and frenzied movements I'd seen previously in other African dances, but centered upon a sinuous, pulsating, rhythmically hypnotizing motion: an instinctive pattern of movements. "The Vulva Dance" was a free flowing form of the feminine. Although choreographed by the dancer herself, the observers were certain (mistakenly) that it was a stylization of traditional African steps.

This was my first introduction to the interpretive dancer, Arisika Razak. Neither small nor thin, the body types usually associated with dancers, Arisika's full female body reflects a spirit and personality filled with grace. A most striking fact about her dancing is that she began at the age of thirty-seven—an age at which most professional dancers are terminating their careers.

As a child Arisika's mother had often called Arisika her "big, clumsy daughter." To this day her mother is shocked and embarrassed that she will accept money for dancing because "as everyone knows, you can't dance." Listening to Arisika tell her story I felt saddened and angered by the damage that she, like so many other people experienced in her childhood. The miracle is that some women like Arisika have gone on to a happy and productive adulthood.

Dance has been an act of liberation for Arisika. She tells women in her dance groups, "Anyone can dance. Don't be intimidated. Dance is language. It is not aerobics, it is moving with spirit."

A year later I met Arisika in her Oakland home where she lives with her teenaged son. As she revealed her life to me, her soft voice belied her strength of character and personal authority. She is not only a professional dancer, she works as a midwife with pregnant women in twelve-hour shifts at the county hospital. ("No one would ever give birth there if they could possibly do anything better.") She expresses sincere empathy for these women: "the ghetto is the psychic underside of a society and fills its nightmares. The ghetto has a life force." This work helps her to remember the danger of arrogance and to remember her roots.

Both physically and spiritually, Arisika's work in dance and midwifery revolves around the female genitalia; as she described it, "the center and creation of ALL life." She believes that it is crucial for women to regain or (in most cases) primarily to establish a sense of themselves and their bodies as beautiful and perfect in their individuality.

As an illustration of this philosophy, Arisika told me a story about a fifty-year-old woman who had seen "The Vulva Dance" and later felt emboldened to ask her husband one day when they were driving in the country to stop and make love to her in an open field. She was astonished at her daring and even more surprised that he said "yes." To Arisika this is the dance at work: dance as a healing force. Dance as Grace.

ARISIKA RAZAK

The key issue for me in my work both as a dancer and as a midwife is the feminine body. There is such a distance that women have from their bodies. My feeling is if you can stand whole in your physical body there is nowhere on earth you cannot stand whole in your being. That's what is important for women to experience.

I have spent countless hours physically examining women, and, after eight years and literally hundreds of exams, I can count on the fingers of maybe two hands, the women who have gotten up on the table, been relaxed and in their bodies. So many women have apologized for how their bodies smelled, so many guard the vulva, even with another woman, covering themselves with their hands. They think that area is sweaty, dirty, to be hidden, bad, ugly. There is so much taboo, shame, and fear.

We think of the sexual parts of our bodies as the most animal parts. They're shameful and dirty to us because primarily they represent animal nature. They are the orifices where fluids flow from, where mucous lives. We aren't comfortable as a culture or as individuals with those issues in our bodies. I mean, the entire cosmetics industry is about changing our scents; it's a testament to that cultural discomfort. So it's important for each of us to reclaim and honor our bodily functions.

Now I realize that it was not always that way. There were times in the past when women honored their bodies. Where women are now is new and temporary. We don't need to hold onto it; it's terribly oppressive. And so I created the Vulva Dance in order to talk about the sacredness of women's genitals, to remind us that women's genitals were once sacred icons. The Sheila-na-gig statue found in Ireland was placed over church doors: the legs are open crosswise while the feet are joined in a diamond shape and the vulva and genitals are prominently, nakedly displayed.

Many of my dance movements come from the sacred postures of women in prehistoric art. In my research I came upon two stories where women had averted a war by "lifting their skirts." Not lying with the men, but by "lifting their skirts," which to me meant displaying an emblem, a reminder that we all come from the same womb, and we all have an obligation to peace.

There's a traditional Aztecan invocation to the goddess of duality which says: "Oh, Golden Flower flowered whose thighs are holy..." Clearly this is the vulva, the sacredness of both sexuality and birthing. We have lost that sacredness as well as the significance of women. Whether we have children or not, if we understand childbirth as a sacred act, we would understand that it is a point of honor to be born in the body of a woman.

I've always felt very close to my sexuality and I think it was one of the doors that opened me to my spirituality. In the early '60s when the first wave of Eastern religions came through this country, I was simply not interested because there was so much emphasis on denying: denying pleasure, the body, desire. And I thought, "I love desire; why would I want to do away with it?" I spend a lot of time dancing in front of mirrors, looking at my body and seeing my body as beautiful, and wanting to share that experience.

Dance allows women to go deep into themselves and let what is empowering come up for them. It is a language: how we speak with spirit, or how spirit speaks us. I'm very opposed to teaching particular steps. Depending on a woman's background, range of motion, physical body type, and weight, she may or may not be able to execute a specific step. What is important is that she experience her body moving in a way that evokes a spiritual center that is deep and that touches core energy within her.

A person with a young, lithe body will be able to extend her legs, point her toes, leap, etc. A woman who weighs 195 pounds, who doesn't exercise, isn't going to do that. It's terribly wrong to think of dancing as aerobics. Dancing is *not* aerobics. Dancing is moving with spirit. There are certain rhythms that we move to which are ours. I tend to come from a very peaceful, harmonious place when I dance. That's the place that I love.

Sometimes I say to women, "Be a tree moving." And they will be the tree with the branches moving furiously in the wind, or they will be the roots going down into the earth—a subtle, slow dance, a very different dance. If they are the wind, are they the furiousness of the wind or the slow breeze? When we dance we experience our inner nature. There is a unity that we can experience moving in dance that is profound and healing and ecstatic. One of the things I've learned from dance is that I can generate ecstasy. That for me is wonderful.

Earlier in my life when I was in New York, I would see old people dancing. Now, the young people would do fancy and difficult steps. The older person might just move their arm, but all their life experiences, all their cultural traditions may be expressed in that simple gesture. All the ways in which a sixty-year-old woman knows that she is still a sexual being will be in her movement. It's different and subtle, but immensely powerful.

So many people are intimidated by dance and feel that they "can't dance." Everyone can dance, everyone can find a place where they not only feel comfortable, but find grace. Grace is really the term. And I like to share that with people when I teach and when I perform. I pray before I dance, every time. It's not so much that the technique be good, but that I move people, that spirit come through the work. Because for me it's not whether my knee bend is straight in the Vulva Dance, but that people open up to a new space and that it move them.

It's interesting that many women viewing the Vulva Dance thought it was a traditional African dance. It isn't. It's a dance I created. It's easy for white women to see Africa as tribal and say to themselves, "Well, this woman can be naked and dance gracefully because that's her tradition." On the contrary, it is *all* of our traditions; all of us as women come from a basic tradition where our naked bodies were sacred, sacred vessels of life and creativity of movement. Sacredness of the union of body and spirit: that's all of our traditions. And it's important for us to reclaim that.

My midwife work is especially important to me because it is a connection to the poor, the disadvantaged. I'm working with women who are cocaine addicts, with women who are sleeping in emergency rooms, with fourteen-year-olds whose parents have kicked them out. I work at the county hospital and nobody goes to the county hospital to deliver if they can do anything better. We only get the people who waited so long that a private doctor won't take them, the people who have MediCal, the women who are illegal aliens.

I saw the movie *Colors* and I respected it because it accurately depicted the world of the ghetto, the world of the gangs. It doesn't glorify the life, it shows the people who are running heroin and cocaine as living in shacks. They're *not* driving Mercedes Benzes and wearing matching jogging suits. They are seventeen-year-olds, half of whom aren't going to make it to twenty-five; they'll be dead by then. I work with the women of men like that, or with the women who are on the fringes of that kind of scene.

What moved me so deeply about the film was the portrayal of how difficult it is to get out of that world. If you're born into it, you don't see any other. There was a study on teenage pregnant girls in Chicago, a small study, but none of the girls knew anyone who had a job, who had gone to college, or who was married. They didn't know *anyone*.

My family doctor, who is a very progressive white man married to a black midwife, said to me once: "Arisika, why don't you create a dance for cocaine-addicted women in East Oakland?" It's a wonderful idea, but my first thought was I can't because I don't know the world. The people who are really going to change how we deal with drugs are people who have been there.

Now I *do* know and understand addiction. I've been in emotionally and sexually addictive relationships. At the core, all addictions come from the same place. The most obscene words are, "I cannot live without you." To be so bonded to someone is an aberration; it's letting go of, losing sight of your own soul and your connection to God or Spirit, admitting you aren't a whole human being. We really are bonded, male and female, to each other, to the extent that we can't stand alone. And I think it's more so for women than for men. Men are socialized, informally, to stand alone. Women are not. And it makes for the worst kind of unhappiness. You see it acted out in the women who stay with men who batter them. There is only one way out, and that is to be able to accept despair as part of a life cycle and to be able to stand whole in the Self.

I have certainly experienced grief with the loss of a loved one, and there is overwhelming grief; I know that. But I also know that fundamentally what it means to be a whole person is to stand *whole*. And that's what the real resolution around addiction is. At the end of Ntozake Shange's play, *For Colored Girls Who Have Considered Suicide/When The Rainbow Is Enuf*, she says, "I found God in myself and I loved Her fiercely."

We have to find sources of love that keep us whole, that sustain us, that don't put us into dependency in situations which are destructive. And that source is inside each of us.

One of the issues that has come up for me in my forties is that of image. I've decided to stop worrying about what people think. I want to be able to state more directly what I feel in the moment as truth regardless of whether it's going to hurt. I don't care as much now about people's opinions because there is only the finiteness of my life; I either do something or I don't. And the only person who feels the consequences is me. This is the power to be unique, to be different from everyone else. One of the things that is traditionally said about older women is that they can do what they want. It's called personal power.

I need to protect myself. I'm clear that I don't have time for friendships or relationships that don't have some spiritual connection. I'm beginning to see that I do want to set limits around me. And I'm beginning to think of where I want to be at sixty. I really want my life to be one of emotional harmony, and I literally have no time for anyone who doesn't bring that into my life.

I have three close, fiftyish women friends and one of them says she can't get enough of her own company. She's delighted to come home and be alone. She says she doesn't even want to think about looking for a relationship. Why, it might take her away from something important like working in her garden! These women are not sexually active in their lives right now for one reason or another, but I just spoke with one of the midwives I work with. She just went and visited her seventy-three-year-old mother who's being someone's mistress now in Florida. She's very sexually active and supposedly her partner made this joke about her being sexually demanding. I think that's great; I aspire to be a sexually demanding sixty- or seventy-year-old!

I want to be dancing at sixty. I want to be dancing Crone dances and I have no idea what they'll be yet. We are redefining our ages. What we saw a generation back in our mothers when they were forty and fifty were women trapped in unhappy marriages, whose creativity had been stuffed back down, who were unable to dance their free selves. Maybe some of the limitations we saw in our mothers' bodies are *not* the limitations of the body, but the manifestations of what their psyches could not handle.

I have been the primary, responsible or nurturing parent for my son. It's been a very grounding experience for me. I started nursing school when he was three and then I went on to public health school, graduate school, and finally midwifery school. In my experience at school, it was the women who had children who did much better than the single women because we really knew why we were there, and it helped us to be more disciplined. I also feel it's very special to be involved in women's spirituality at the same time that I am raising a male child as a single parent. It feels like a special responsibility. I care about that and I have a very good relationship with my son.

I've been weaving it all together: being a parent, a dancer, a midwife, a black woman in so many white circles, a peace-maker. Together they ground me and make me rich. The discipline of dealing with my son and the sacrifices I make to put aside what I want to do because of what my kid needs carry over to how I approach the dance. The way that I forgive my son is the way that I forgive myself for pushing my knees too hard. There is an ability to be more patient with my body and that's important. It all stirs together.

I have learned methods for taking care of myself. Periodically I will buy about five science fiction novels and devour them, just spend an entire day-and-a-half reading in every spare moment. I find that this helps my psyche get through tired, or lonely, or difficult periods. I always know it will pass.

That's one of the delights of the forties—I've had enough life experiences, enough joy and pain, to know that they just keep turning. They will both continue to be there and I have some choice about what I do with them.

I feel that I'm a whole person, I'm at peace with myself. There is a lot of joy in my life, and some of that is literally by the grace of God, and some of it is worked for and earned, if you will, or paid for in some way: in time, pain, discipline, or experience. Where I am now has been paid for. There is a part of me that believes that everything you get you pay for. Everything is worked for. Everything is earned psychically.

My current view of the world is that life really is the braided streams of light and darkness, joy and pain, and I just accept that. They both exist and I walk both of them. I used to say that my life was like dancing on the edges of blades of grass, but since my forties it's not like that anymore. It's gotten easier. I don't want it to be that hard anymore. I've done that.

It isn't as if it were a conscious decision or something; it's been the grace of God. I really feel that my life is graced. I mean, I'm one in a million. People who had the kind of abuse I received as a child don't come out whole. I really believe in the grace of God. And I dance. I danced at a winter solstice gathering one year and I literally felt grace enter the room and I knew the dance was going to be perfect. I don't even mean that it was me so much. I just understood what happens when grace fills you; it's a palpable quality, and it's healing.

There's been a lot of grace in my life. When I was seventeen I was given my name. And the name Arisika means "Joy of the Peaceful Union." ■

The forties are fragile—I have to remember my reading glasses when I go out. Thank God I wasn't a movie star. I was called to be a healer, a wounded healer, someone who has fallen apart and put herself back together again.

—Gabrielle Roth

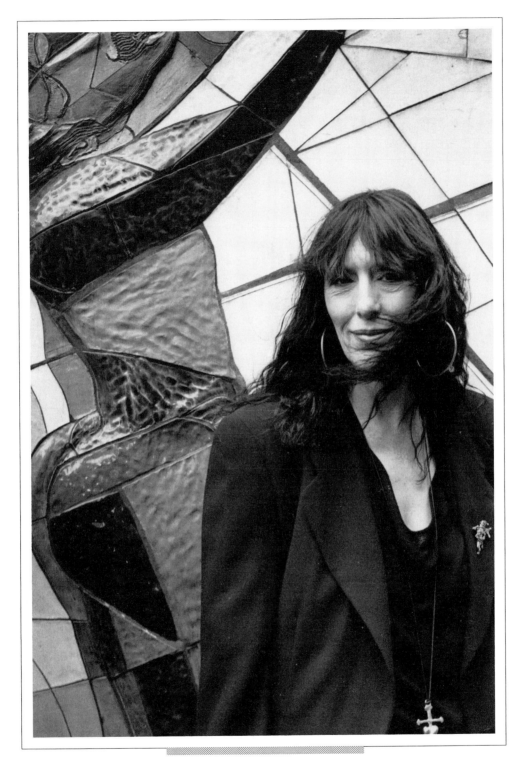

Gabrielle Roth

• P R O F I L E •

URBAN: 1. of, pertaining to, or comprising a city or town.
2. living in a city.
3. characteristic of or accustomed to cities.

SHAMAN: 1. medicine man, or person with magical powers.
2. ability to communicate with spirits through trances and rituals.
3. shamans ward off evil, heal, and, in some cases, tell the future.
4. ability to interchange form or shape with animals.

Gabrielle Roth's first book, *Maps to Ecstasy: Teachings of an Urban Shaman*, describes her unique style of shamanic healing with people. In workshops and seminars presented throughout the world, Gabrielle challenges, cajoles, seduces and encourages the participants' authenticity to come out and dance. In her presence no one is too old, too young, too big, too little, or too awkward to reach deep inside, feel the pulse of life and let it move. Through exercises, dance, song, poetry, meditation, theatre, and ritual, Gabrielle shares her life's work and explores how shamanic principles can be incorporated into our contemporary, urban lives. Her work is stripped of much of the indigenous attributes of shamanism, but not of its core energies: she rock and rolls her way to ecstasy, while teaching others how to do the same.

I first experienced Gabrielle's work only two weeks after my father died. Several months earlier I'd enrolled in the upcoming three-day workshop and at that moment had no idea how timely it would become for me. Much of Gabrielle's work focuses on our life cycles, a large and important part of which is to become reconciled with our parents as they actually were (or have remained) and to release the fantasy of either the perfect parent or the entirely toxic parent. Somewhere in between lies the truth. My weekend with Gabrielle helped me to arrive at a resolution with the memory of a man with whom I'd been estranged for most of my forty-one years.

In a large group of well over 100 people, each participant felt the presence of Gabrielle. Indeed, each person enjoyed a warm and individual recognition. People came from throughout the United States with enormous expectations. Each one purged their way through the weekend and left filled with the best of themselves, unencumbered by tired and wasted dreams, ready to embark with renewed energy—psychologically, physically and spiritually—on a new life journey. As individuals we dared to venture out of the safe cocoons—inertia and imitation—and leap into the world of movement and imagination.

Nearly one year later I met with Gabrielle in her Greenwich Village home near Parsons School of Design and New York University. Her loft is one of the most spectacular I've seen in Manhattan, flooded with natural light through a wall of windows, and expansive enough in which to pursue ecstatic dance and perform ritual theatre. It is filled with photos of Gabrielle (taken by Robert, her photographer/attorney husband of fourteen years), a variety of folk art, including several over-sized Huichol Yarn Paintings hung on the walls, and a collection of percussive instruments that Ginger Baker and Olatunji would envy.

Gabrielle is slender by anyone's standards, with the strong yet fluid body of a dancer. Her hair, raven black, is set against the white pallor of an alabaster face which seldom sees the sun amid New York's skyscrapers. Hers is a beautifully soulful face, perfect for a subterranean Anne Rice novel, with hazel eyes that are intelligent and mischievous. Using her entertaining wit and sense of irony, Gabrielle revealed that many years ago when she lived and taught movement at Esalen in Big Sur, California, she pitied the pale New Yorkers who came to the California coast in search of both sunny days and inner illumination. Now she is one of them.

Painfully familiar with the dilemmas of anorexia, Gabrielle was anorexic for the better (or worse) part of her teenage years. She believes that anorexia is a body/spirit split, and is a symbol of our times. She managed to be released from it when she moved to Europe where she stayed for some years. During this time Gabrielle became her own person, "broke through sexually" and decided to take responsibility for her own body and her own needs and do exactly what she wanted to do. Gabrielle works with many anorexic women, helping them find that place of independence within themselves and discover the sacred celebration of their female bodies.

Gabrielle Roth has been deeply in touch with the spirit world and it has been her major source of identification throughout her life. The raven, considered in Greek mythology to possess oracular capabilities, is Gabrielle's power animal; and appropriately, through the course of our interview, I often mar-

veled at her bird-like grace and quick-as-lightening movements. Her feather/
hands became a phenomenal blur of wings and talons: the shaman—shape
shifting.

GABRIELLE ROTH

I was raised in a very simple and loving family in San Francisco. I had a traditional mother who stayed at home and took care of her children, and a father who went off to work every morning. They were young parents, passionate about each other, affectionate and tender with their kids.

I felt covered, until my father nearly died of cancer when he was thirty-two. He recovered, but his illness was a traumatic experience for me and my family. I realized, for the first time, that I could lose something I truly loved, that Fate could twist and turn and leave me without a dad. And his long stay in the hospital put us on the financial edge. I learned to survive. I learned not to take things for granted. And most importantly, through it all, I was surrounded by guardian angels, spirit animals and talking trees.

Through them I created my own relationship to God. It was much more dynamic than the Catholic version. I like ritual, but dogma leaves me cold. It doesn't dance. It doesn't change when the music changes. Dogma didn't move me. And I had to dance.

I always danced, I loved to dance. I still love to dance. Dancing is my prayer. I dance when I'm happy, sad, angry, afraid. It's my mother tongue. It is always spiritual for me because I worship the spirit of the dance, not its form. To dance deeply is to breathe deeply, to be in touch with the invisible force that connects and moves us all. To surrender to the dance, to enter its beat and trance, to let it fly, free form, to find unity in moving my body, to express my heart and empty my mind—this is ecstasy, the place where the contraries dissolve and something else is ignited, something deeper, something divine. And this ecstatic dance is the foundation of all my work.

I was never much for transcendence. Every time I lifted myself above it all, it was all still there when I came back down. Transformation: no way out but through.

My deepest exploration has been to map this journey I dance from inertia to ecstasy. It's difficult to talk about ecstasy; it only happens in emptiness, and for me that emptiness follows a wild, totally abandoned, sweaty dance. Here I meet God, not as an abstraction, not as some philosophical possibility, not as some pie-in-the-sky promise, but as a direct experience. A real, concrete, tangible marriage of spirit and flesh, of *my* spirit to *my* flesh.

I was conditioned otherwise. I was told I couldn't have God and sex in the same body. What a choice. I went for God. "Anorexia," they call it now. I didn't have a name for it then; all I knew was that I had to punish my body for having "those" feelings. It was simple—if I didn't feed my body, it wouldn't grow. So that's what I did. I starved my woman.

I healed myself without even knowing I was ill. I had to learn how to love my body, express my emotions and free my mind from the bondage of its conditioning. I did it dancing. I did it by accepting myself, accepting the shape, height and weight of the body I was born into with all of its rhythms, feelings, wants, aches, needs, warts, wounds and blessings. My body, the shape of my consciousness, handmade American, one-of-a-kind, a work-in-progress, my unfinished symphony. My home. Where I live and where I will die. My body.

So maybe it weighs more than I want it to. Maybe my hips are too wide. Maybe my hair's too thin. Maybe that's just the way it is. And, that's the me I've got to love—and shop for. Might as well get behind what I've got.

It's not easy to find support for this attitude in a culture that denies physical reality, honors conformity in a world of rich diversity, and fears change in the name of security. It's tough to be who you are. I had to fight for the right to be me. And in discovering that I am now, have always been and will always be in process, I found my healing.

This is a value I've tried to pass on to my son. He is on his way to Hawaii to be a surfer. Some of my friends freaked out. Jonathan is twenty-one; what about college, security, the future? I blessed his leaving. It's his life, his dreams, his passion. Who am I to know more than he does about the through line to his destiny? And what better teacher than the ocean, the Great Mother, to deliver the lessons in humility, respect, balance and surrender that he'll need to flourish. I trust him. I trust her. Riding her waves, he'll discover his own.

What better place to learn survival skills than in the context of his own dreams! I know the pain of others' experiences. So many people pass through my workshops who lived out their parents' dream instead of their own. I've seen the pain when they later get a glimpse of what they've given up to do so—their power, their passion, their gifts. Forty is a little late to ride a surfboard for the first time. It's late to do a lot of things—but not too late.

Actually, I learned a lot more from Jonathan than I ever taught him. Being a mother is an important part of my spiritual training. There's no way to "transcend" this one, not when he needs his three a.m. feeding, not when he's going off to Hawaii to surf twenty-foot waves. He has taught me unconditional love and been my clearest mirror. He has taught me to walk my talk.

As I move deeper into my maturity, I am blessed with a deep, long-term, beautifully-grounded relationship with my husband. We raised our kids together. We've buried our fathers, had our homes, our animals, shared bluejeans, been up and down together and separately, and survived the roller coaster of hundreds of creative projects.

All this while running the gamut from living and working together twenty-four hours a day seven days a week for three years straight to the last fifteen months when I've spent twelve of them on the road.

People say, "How can you handle the separation?" We don't. We're never really separated in the sense that the relationship is ever at question. I married my soulmate—"us" is a psychic given. Even when I am madly shopping in London and he's pouting in New York. Or I'm freaking out about being alone in a hotel room during the outbreak of a war in the Persian Gulf and he's at home in Manhattan playing drums. It all seems to work.

I also love my work. I'm a professional ecstatic. I go to work with the sole purpose of reaching ecstasy. I don't always get there, but it's a lot more about the going than the getting there. It's my fascination to break down the steps to ecstasy, to find my way in and out of trance, and to do this, I have to be able to know and outsmart my own patterns of resistance as well as those of everybody else. It's my job.

I know the swamp of the ego, but I'm hooked on turning my suffering into art. Poison into poems. Tears into tracks. I sweat memories and shift realities between my bones. Bones that aren't growing any younger. My dance is getting better though; it's deeper and I'm more inside it—less of me and more of the dance. This is my art, my practice. I expect to die dancing.

Aging can be fluid, and graceful, and funny even though it hurts, since death is the door prize. In indigenous cultures, shamans don't reach their potential until their fifties. It is expected that they will grow into their power, not out if it. I like this concept.

I am going to die—at least my body will. In fact, it is dying as we speak. Process. Nothing to do but surrender to the bittersweet pull of this dance. I knew I was grown up when I hit forty and tried to hide from death. The forties are fragile—I have to remember my reading glasses when I go out. Thank God I wasn't a movie star. I wanted to be an actress but was called to be a healer, a wounded healer, someone who has fallen apart and put herself back together again.

Fear of my own body. Denial of its needs. Hatred of its parts. Distrust of its messages. This was my disease and discomfort. My dismemberment was psychic and brutal, my wings broken, my spirit exiled. I had to heal myself. And in the process I have ritualized this healing for others. There's been no turning back.

I am on a path, a mission to find my true self. Who is she? What does it mean that she is a she? And that she is a shaman. What does all this mean, I ask myself? It's been painful being a female shaman with no traditions, no roots, no real models in a patriarchal Western culture, a culture that burned the answers to all my questions at the stake. Thousands of healers, mostly women. Burned and buried.

I am part of a tradition rising from these ashes. Lifting my head above my own pain long enough to see the light inside this darkness. And to translate it into a dance. One that rocks and rolls from inside out.

Unlike a shaman in the wilderness or on the desert plains, I live in a loft in Manhattan and often spend my nights in places like recording studios using technology to record the trance and translate my maps into music, into beats per minute. Trance dance music for ecstasy junkies, the real thing, no pills please.

Shamanism is indigenous to its culture, a specific manifestation of forces at work at a given place and time. Shamans have a great deal in common regardless of time and space. Their techniques are universal and 75,000 years old. Market tested, you could say. An Australian Aboriginal, an Eskimo, a Siberian, a Huichol or an urban-modern model like myself—we all use the same basic tools, like the beat.

I use the beat to seduce souls back into their bodies. I have my theatrics; all shamans have their theater together—the spell they will cast to seduce the spirit into the body. And that theatre has to do with the mythology of the shaman's culture.

The mythology of my culture is "Chorus Line"—being discovered as the most fascinating person you know. I guess in my work I help people to do this. It has always been natural for me to catalyze energy into motion and motion into maps—patterns of possibilities. I've been doing this in one way or another since I was eleven years old.

I've been making maps down the yellow brick roads. And all these maps add up to a cosmology—a map of the psyche: how it is formed, wounded and healed. It took thirty years for me to articulate it and I'm still its student. I make maps to transform cultural and personal neuroses into creative forms, like dance, music, poetry, rituals and theater pieces. And all these forms represent the times and tones of a place and a people. My time. My place. My people.

In my writing I have attempted to articulate the awakening of the shamanic archetype in each of us. This archetype is an unusual concoction of dancer, singer, poet, actor and healer. Put all these ingredients in one blender and shake them up—let them move and the result is as unique as the soul. It *is* the soul and the soul is the shamanic part of us.

We have shamans in Western culture, whether they know it or not. Sam Sheppard, Joe Chaikin, Robin Williams, Mickey Hart, Lily Tomlin, Peter Gabriel, Susan Boulet—people who use their creative energy to transform the pain of a culture into personal art. Could I have come this far without Ernestine?

My work is giving space to the creative spirit—learning to get out of its way and be in its service at the same time. Whenever someone is in touch with their creativity, with their own powers and gifts, and when all of this is grounded in their true self, then all neurotic baggage drops away until it becomes background rather than foreground. I've seen it again and again. I say follow your fantasies into reality.

We are all responsible for the manifestation of our soul power, our destiny, our gifts, our dreams. We have to dance our dreams awake in this plane, on this planet. That is our contribution to the whole, whether it is being a mother, a dressmaker, a politician, a toll-collector, a shaman or a rock 'n' roll singer. We each have responsibility to express ourselves. And in this expression is the key to our healing. ■

Because we are in our forties is not a reason to be depressed. *Imagine if this were your last day, how would you live it* . . . and live differently.

—Mayumi Oda

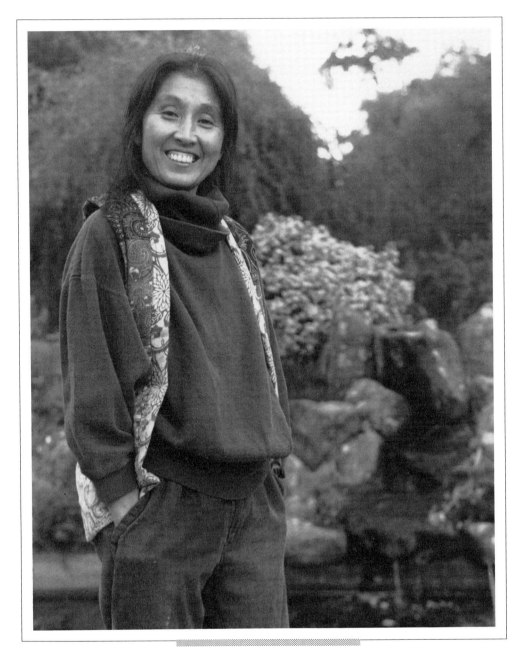

Mayumi Oda

• P R O F I L E •

The Chinese definition for the fortieth decade is "Standing Alone." When interpreting this symbol, one can read "Standing Alone" as being alone or lonely, or as being strong and independent. It can also be part of both, for an independent person is sometimes one who is alone and vulnerable. I found this an accurate characterization of the women I interviewed—independent and potent, and simultaneously vulnerable and often solitary.

Mayumi Oda describes herself as an independent person living alone, but one who is not lonely. An internationally respected artist, Mayumi resides in the beautifully verdant sea inlet which sits like an emerald on the edge of Muir Beach, California. She paints, gardens, meditates, writes, cooks, drinks tea, and visits with a steady stream of friends and admirers. The lush, fecund, nurturing coastal region bears familiar contours found in many of the archetypal goddess figures painted by Mayumi, images of the maternal universe.

One early October afternoon I drove to Marin County, through Mill Valley and past Green Gulch Zen Center, to interview Mayumi Oda. After five years of committed work by numerous craftsmen and gardeners, her home has become an artists' paradise with a large studio space ensconced in glass which overlooks part of the expansive grounds. The house is surrounded by flourishing gardens, allowing one to take a leisurely, meditative walk entirely around it. Each door of the house opens out onto a landscaped vignette: an exquisite pond for carp, or a living Ikebana flower arrangement, a fruit orchard or patch of vegetables, perhaps a secluded shrine of the Buddha. Adorning the interior white walls of her home are a variety of ethnic arts, traditional Japanese woodblock prints and antique furniture pieces, contemporary hand-crafts, and a sampling of Mayumi's paintings and serigraphs.

There is an energy or mood which inhabits certain dwellings. Such a quality is palpable in Mayumi's home and she has named it: Spirit of the Valley. This title was inspired by a passage from the *Tao Te Ching*:

> The spirit of the valley never dies.
> It is called the mysterious female.
> Gateway of the creating force.

It flows continuously.
Use will never drain it.

As an artist, Mayumi has experienced great success and has had numerous one-woman shows in Japan and on both coasts of the United States. She has also had good fortune as an author with her books, *Goddesses* (1981), and *Happy Veggies* (1988), which is a joyful celebration of the profusion and multiplicity of life in a vegetable garden, a bow in reverence to the ecosystem of the earth.

Her Japanese heritage has influenced her art and she poetically explained that:

> I made my goddesses to explore Japanese traditional design, which is so free, extravagant and sometimes even wild. Goddesses started to play in the flowering fields of kimono brocade and swim in oceans of Hokusai waves. My free female figures brought old designs into the present.

These full-bodied godddesses, imbued with strength, vitality, and an unmistakable independence, seem to command their space. Mayumi believes she began painting these goddesses because they were the qualities which she herself wished to embody. The influence of the Japanese writer, Raicho Hiratsuka, on Mayumi's art is expressed in Raicho's evocative plea:

> Women, please let your sun, your concentrated energy, your own submerged authentic vital power shine out from you.

Mayumi's art is integrated into her daily life, it encircles her gardening and childrearing, it is embraced by her meditation and the simple act of preparing and drinking tea. The ultimate importance of each action in every day is typified and honored by her. Mayumi's behavior is mindful and in harmony with her environment.

If I could describe Mayumi Oda in one word that word would be "integrated." I have met few others whose lives so seamlessly interlaced their primary concerns and philosophical discourse into their daily routine. The apparent ease of her existence masks the decades of disciplined Buddhist meditation which Mayumi credits for the "freedom" she now feels pervades her life. "It didn't happen overnight," she modestly reminded me. For Mayumi, a woman who survived the horrors of war in Japan, the importance of peace has been an unbroken thread weaving her personal and professional lives together.

I was born near Tokyo before the Hiroshima bombing. As a result, for perhaps the first ten years of my early childhood, I had a fear of war and bombing, of not having enough food and clothing, and of not having any toys to play with. Now I'm grateful for those experiences, because I learned to entertain myself with very little. I have many things, but I don't feel the need for them.

The Japan of my childhood was very different from contemporary Japan. My mother came from an artistic, upper-class family. She did flower arrangements, and she taught me the tea ceremony. She showed us how to make things with our hands. In those days parents weren't so busy and she spent hours and hours making clothes for me and the rest of my family. The making of things was very important, because there was no other means of getting them. If we wanted something, we made it. We didn't call it creativity. It was really out of necessity—we needed sweaters and socks and we had to be resourceful. When you make a hat or a bathing suit, it gives you a certain basic confidence in yourself and your life. My childhood provided that confidence for me.

I used to say to people who were demonstrating for nuclear freeze, "Do you *really* understand what the bomb is?" People in America don't understand. When you come from a culture that remembers how people died and suffered, you know that we are in desperate need of peace. It is absolutely horrible to live in war. As a three-year-old I was separated from my father when I had to evacuate with my mother and brother. My family did not die in the bombings, but I saw people dying right and left around me.

Japan should know what is so terrible about war. Instead, they have the most nuclear plants, and have become an incredibly consuming culture.

Their material deprivation after World War II deeply affected them and it is going to take a while for them to realize their own tradition.

I was born into a Buddhist family and had quite a serious religious upbringing as a child. It was not exactly Zen, although my father was a Zen scholar. My grandparents belonged to a different kind of sect. They practiced chanting at home. At one point I wanted to get away from that, and as a teenager I worked hard to rebel against it.

In my early twenties, right after college, I married an American man who was a Japanese literature student at the University of Japan. I thought, "I can get away from my family's traditions; I'm not Japanese anymore."

Later, when I came to New York and went through the '60s, I saw many things happening around me, and I needed to make peace with myself. At that time I went back to find my roots, and they came to me very naturally. I began meditation. And, somehow, having the perspective of living abroad and away from my own culture, I didn't feel bound by it. The Japanese culture can include oppressive traditions, but now I didn't have a need to see it that way.

We lived in New York, Princeton, and Cambridge where my husband taught at the universities. It was through this association that I became involved in the women's movement. By the early '70s I felt that something was lacking and what we needed was the liberation of us all. It wasn't enough to blame men and society for our problems.

After giving birth to my sons I felt tremendous inner strength and power. In the process I realized there was some key to being a woman. It definitely tapped my inner resources. That life-giving force that we have as women created a tremendous alchemical process which, I think, transformed me from a little girl into a woman. It was very, very powerful and changed my thinking.

I began to look inwardly, to find out who I was, rather than seeking something outside myself. I didn't know it at the time, but it was a turning toward spirituality. I started to paint the goddesses. At first I didn't call them goddesses; they were more like archetypes such as the Earth Mother. But I recognized that the potential power we have as women wanted to be expressed.

I think the creative process is not about creating something else; it's about the process itself creating who *I* am. In other words, I create myself through my creation, through my creative activity. I had a tremendous urge to create certain things. So I went back and thought "why?" It became clear to me after I finished writing my first book called *Goddesses*. I realized, my Goddess! This is what I want to be, so I have created it. But then that process became completely a process of transformation: you are always opening the door to the next level, to unknown places. Creativity is not a driving force. It happens. It creates itself. And you have to be open.

It's wonderful to have morning tea, and then have an idea or image come. Many artists are driven painters; they're born to paint. I'm not like that. I produce enough, I think. People tend to say I'm driven to draw. I don't think so. Life to me is like exploring things I haven't seen before, the places where I haven't been. My father used to say, "God, your curiosity drives me crazy." To see something I haven't seen, to experience that sense of wonder—almost the magic—of everything, to be able to see the magic: that's part of being an artist.

When I was married I supported a good portion of my family, and certainly since I've been separated and been on my own, I've supported myself. I'm lucky. Many artists do wonderful work, but cannot make a living by it. My work is not good or bad; it has a quality that people like and they are willing to support me. Maybe it's like buying a good luck charm or something. I am lucky that I never had to struggle financially.

So I try to work with people who are having harder times. It's difficult when you have to struggle to sell your art and make a living.

The one thing I would have done differently in my life would have been to raise my children more consciously. I had them when I was young. I just didn't know. If I knew then what I know now, I would have done it differently. I was not a total mother to my children. I enjoyed being a mother, but often I regretted the time I wasn't doing my art because I had to take care of the kids. Kids are pretty flexible; they become wonderful children. In some ways my sons now appreciate that I wouldn't be a total mother to them.

In a sense I feel that children are borrowed. They stay with you for fifteen or sixteen years and you do your best to equip them and then send them out into the world. I'm trying to do that as much as possible for my one son who is still with me before he leaves the nest. You pass on what you've learned in your life so they can take it out into the world.

Because my father was a professional teacher, he had a profound intellectual and spiritual influence on my life. My relationships with men are usually like that. Someone I love will bring me something I have not experienced and open my brain or consciousness.

There are two women who inspired me the most, two Japanese writers. One was Raicho Hiratsuka, a Zen practitioner who became a mother figure for women's liberation in Japan. The other is Kanoko Okamoto, who studied Tantric Buddhism and wrote colorful, passionate novels. She inspired me a great deal. These women were both non-conformists and independent from tradition. However, even if these women had not existed, I would probably have lived my life the way I wanted to live it—I was determined.

But it is comforting to know that someone has done it before you and in more difficult situations. While I live in this country because it is much easier for me, I admire the women who stayed in my country and lived as non-conformists.

In order to heal the difficult wound between the male and the female, I think both men and women must learn receptivity. This is the hardest thing for me to do. As women we felt we were taken advantage of and so we gave up being receptive. We have equated it with passivity, but receptivity usually takes tremendous strength. That's what I am trying to cultivate for myself.

At the same time, it is interesting to look at this aggressive power I created in my goddesses. I developed my male side. It's no longer only the male who is very aggressive; we have also developed our aggressive side. I think of receptivity as right action: sometimes you need to be receptive, sometimes you need to be active, and sometimes you can be both. You have to be receptive to inspiration. Receiving the inspiration and then producing the output work together. It's basically the balance, the integration of both.

What makes me happy is going beyond my boundary. Breaking my boundary, my small self grows larger and is able to meet others completely, to be helpful to others. I do not exist alone. Being helpful permeates, I hope, every speck of my life. It's how I like to live. It is the way I eat, the way I breathe, the way I dress, the away I connect to people and work with them in peace and harmony.

I think I am much happier than when I was in my thirties. Life is easier, much more enjoyable. Because we are in our forties is not a reason to be depressed. Imagine if this were your last day, how would you live it . . . *and live differently.* My grandmother always sewed, and toward the end of her life she couldn't see very well. She would begin a new kimono and she would say, "This will be my last one." And then while sewing it she'd say, "Hmm, I have time to sew one more." ■

In my thirties I acted impulsively, without thought—this was wonderful and much of my work is reflective of that energy. In a woman's forties, however, there is more questioning and more responsibility for what you put out to the world.

—Barbara Hammer

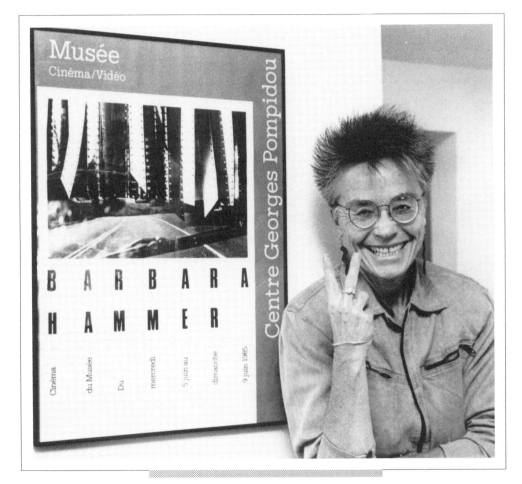

Barbara Hammer

Often a person working in the arts must leave her home base in order to make it in another city or even another country. Such was the case for Laurie Anderson look-alike Barbara Hammer who, as an experimental filmmaker, felt that she had been identified only as a lesbian artist in San Francisco (where she first began making films in her early thirties), rather than as an artist with perceptual interests contributing to the general culture. So ten years ago she made the big move to Manhattan and has remained bi-coastal since then. Barbara receives a great deal of emotional nourishment from the natural world, and also needs the mental stimulation offered by art museums and galleries. Living in Oakland and Manhattan, she feels, feeds her both spiritually and mentally.

Barbara's maternal grandmother, a cook for D.W. Griffith, was her earliest artistic influence and was the first to give Barbara the permission and encouragement to "do what you want to do, Barbie." In between her jobs as a domestic cook (due to her iconoclastic personality, she was fired quite frequently), Barbara's grandmother, Anna Kusz, would end up living in the Hammer household every six months. At the kitchen table Anna would construct sculptures "out of anything." She would paint with oil paints on styrofoam meat–packaging cartons; and setting a beautiful table would be a work of art to her. Having a grandmother who was a co-conspirator in the making of art, Barbara learned firsthand that art is anything you say it is, and the most important decision is to continue to make it. She remains deeply grateful to her grandmother's influence and especially appreciative because she can now recognize the impossible odds against women in her grandmother's time to fulfill their personal dreams.

Barbara's mother also influenced her daughter, but differently. When Barbara was a precocious, brown-haired, green-eyed, freckle-faced little girl in Hollywood during the forties, another dimpled darling was making more money than any other woman in show business: the child star Shirley Temple. Coming from an immigrant, Ukranian background, Marian Hammer had a powerful desire to rise above the working class . . . and Barbara was the answer. Due to a lack of available finances for the *de rigueur* child acting classes, the fantasy was never realized. But Barbara's natural proclivity toward the theatre arts has remained with her. Her mother died before Barbara became a filmmaker and she muses that, "It would be very curious for her to see that I am involved in film—but on the other side of the camera."

Completing her studies in psychology at UCLA, Barbara was married the day after graduation. Her one regret is that she "had only a single day of independence" between her graduation and the day of her marriage. She now understands how vitally important that period is for a woman in which "she can make her own way in the world, earning money, traveling, having an experience as a solitary individual, rather than as a child of a family, or the wife of a husband."

Moving to the San Francisco Bay Area with her husband, Barbara enrolled in the Masters' Program in the English literature department at San Francisco State University. Several years later she worked with emotionally disturbed adolescents but eventually came to realize that an important part of her was not being expressed—the artist. Without a particular art form in which to direct her yearning for creativity she felt that she simply "wanted to stay home and *make things*. But I couldn't justify the self-indulgence." As so often happens with young women, the urge to create was sublimated into the most obvious and ostensibly practical route: pregnancy. "So, I tried to get pregnant. Luckily, we were unable to conceive. I say luckily because what I *really* wanted was to be an artist."

In response to the question of how she initially became interested in film making, Barbara recalled, "When I first saw Maya Deren's *Meshes in the Afternoon*, I knew there was a cinema for me to make." She feels "...lucky to be alive at the same time that so many wonderful women filmmakers are working like Gunvor Nelson, and Yvonne Rainier." While talking with Barbara Hammer about her experimental films, I sensed that she feels a serious responsibility to her life's work, as if she were continuing the lineage of many fine women directors; she is a link into the future of women's experimental filmmaking. I also have considerable respect for her as an artist, for experimental film seems to me the poetry of cinema. A poet or an experimental filmmaker does not expect (and seldom receives) the professional recognition, or financial remuneration reserved for the successful novelist or the feature film director. However, they continue with their work, either through passion or compulsion, or a combination of both.

On her fortieth birthday Barbara celebrated with a massive happy birthday/ farewell party, after which she soon made her move to New York. During the party she screened her newly completed film called *Dream Age*, which was her first cinematic statement about aging. In the film a woman is seen hiking around San Francisco, meeting various parts of herself: a wise underground woman, a seductress—who leads her astray—a crone in her seventies, a guardian angel who gives her what she needs. All are gray-haired and at peace with themselves and their aging process.

When Barbara spoke about her fantasy of aging, she conjured an image of herself as "an eccentric old woman," an archetype inspired by a photograph of a white-haired woman sitting on a BMW motorcycle which she saw many years ago in Stuttgart, Germany, where she was teaching English and women's studies in Stuttgart American High School. "My ideal scenario is that I will be driving this *machine* and the older I get, the faster I'll go." With the igniting electricity of intelligence and curiosity sparking from her spiked hair, it is a likely projection.

BARBARA HAMMER

I became both a lesbian and an artist when I was thirty, so I always saw my thirties as my adolescent period. This was my time for growing up as a woman in the world—a woman relating to women, a woman relating to the world, and a woman making art. I didn't feel middle-aged in my forties as these were the years that began my mature period. As an older woman, I have a sense of knowing myself more, and knowing which of my works are really valuable. Earlier, I could make anything and convince myself that it was good work. Now I know what deserves attention, commitment and completion, and what is a passing idea that has merit but doesn't deserve a place-setting at the table.

In my thirties I acted impulsively, without thought—this was wonderful and much of my work is reflective of that energy. In a woman's forties, however, there is more questioning and more responsibility for what is put out to the world.

Society determines the construction of the meaning of age. What will be interesting and probably infuriating is what Baba Copper calls "the invisible sixties," when women feel as if they are put in a black box and no one recognizes their sixty years of growth and wisdom. Instead, they are discounted as people without a history (little, old, helpless ladies). I think of the Gray Panthers and other elder activist groups and I know I will be one of the tigers out there growling.

I am also infuriated by the ageist remarks I hear: "You don't look your age", or "You're so young for your age." These comments, based on youth-oriented culture, are pervasive, insidious, and undermining. Our society is so completely permeated by this thinking that even feminists and other political leaders of both sexes make such remarks.

My film *Double Strength* made in 1978, depicts a relationship between a woman ten years older and me. She was forty-eight at the time with a strong face showing some wrinkles. Many of my other films also feature older women. In Europe the audiences felt these films were feminist in the sense that I didn't idealize or romanticize a body or a face even though these were images of my lovers. I think an older woman is a beautiful woman.

I recently interviewed a seventy-five-year-old woman. She said something about aging that rings true to me. She said, "You don't feel that you are aging, because you always feel like the same person you were when you were thirteen. For example, I know my eyelids are drooping. I'm very much aware of my skin, but I don't *feel* my own wrinkles. When I go to the mirror I see an older face, but I remain the same person inside. Although there is less physical energy, there is a core or personality that has that same energy as the thirteen-year-old."

My latest film *Sanctus* (1990) uses recently found footage of moving X-rays of the human body shot by Dr. James Sibley Watson and his colleagues in the fifties. Watson is considered one of the fathers of American avant-garde film. I found this footage in the George Eastman House in Rochester, New York in a silver can labeled "Watson's X-rays." They were on 35mm nitrate film. No one had looked at them since they had been placed there decades before. I was the first to have this opportunity.

I then began to research Dr. Watson himself. I found that he had started The Dial Press, the first press to publish the poet Marianne Moore in this country. He was also a philanthropist who built the Rochester Art Museum and funded college educations for several people. Later he helped refine cinefluorography, a method of using fluoroscopes and radiation to image the interior of the human body for diagnostic purposes.

In *Sanctus* I show Watson's Xrays of a moving human body, when it is fragile and immune system dysfunctions are prevalent. We are forced to look beyond the surface to find a deeper meaning and the film restores the sense of fragility and spirituality to the human body. We are confronted with CFIDS, AIDS, cancer and pollution: all the breakdowns of the systems that haven't been protected.

We don't recognize that we are skeletons with these very fragile yet strong organs encased in this protective framework. A few years before I started this film I made a video using a skeleton as an attempt to reach down to the bare bones of life and the aging process. I want to feel my skeleton, to know that I'm losing cells, and to know what my systems are doing inside. The body is a miracle, and knowledge of it makes me live more deeply rather than think of myself as a flesh form to cover with clothes.

I don't place any authority on any configuration outside myself like a god or a goddess. However, I did have what I call a "spirituality period," when I made goddess films and even called my film company Goddess Films. That seemed to be a short-lived period when the matriarchal goddesses were being re-examined by archaeologists and historians, like Merlin Stone and Charlene Spretnak, among others. After a few years this no longer held interest for me as I find much of goddess work redundant and not really creative. It seems to re-echo an image, much as Catholicism re-echoes another image.

To me *imagination* is what is spiritual, what is renewing. The creative process *is* a spiritual process. I am filled by looking at other people's creative work, and I am especially stimulated when I don't understand it. I might begin to understand it but I am led into it more and more because it is not totally apparent to me the first time. Why should it be? When we meet someone it takes years to get to know them. It takes years to develop one's art. Why should it be available at first glance. Good work requires multiple viewing and reading.

A reward for my work is when someone responds to what I make. After working alone in my studio for nine months I bring my project out into the world. When the viewer's response meets the artist's intention, that is spiritual, that's a communion, then I'm speaking. Perhaps this is what is spiritual: two people talking to one another, engaging and listening to the other.

I think I make films as a way to communicate what I can't say in words. I need the images, I need the sound, I need the rhythm of the structure, and then I need a darkened room where all the focus is on the projection. The response of the audience makes the film live and is a form of communication.

This is similar to communicating with my creative process while working on the optical printer, communicating with space in nature when I am hiking, or communicating with another during intimate talks. Those are all little nuclei of the spirit. So often "spirituality" is a hackneyed word and doesn't feel appropriate for the specific moments which touch me.

My purpose is to be as honest as I can and to recognize all the social constructions which have formed me. I have learned from post-modern criticism and semiology that the way we look at the world is determined by constructions. Among the most basic is gender construction which is not innate but applied to our institutions. It keeps me humble to realize that much of who I am was shaped by my mother, by the high school I attended, and by the lesbian culture that I came out in.

When I came out in the seventies it was the exciting time when the second wave of feminism hit. For me, it was the first wave. I was at a community college teaching English and a communications class. A group of women began meeting on the campus in conjunction with a women's studies class. After school ended we continued to meet and

The Santa Rosa Women's Liberation Society was formed. I became involved in the dramatic or theatrical section of that group of women.

During these meetings, one of the women said she was a lesbian. At the age of thirty I had never heard the "L" word. What does that say about education in the United States? *The New York Times* did not print the word lesbian until the late 1920's, but it still wasn't used in the high school or universities that I attended. I was very fascinated with what the word meant so I asked this self-proclaimed dyke to explain it. She said that being a lesbian meant loving women and caring for them, and, in particular, one woman. I thought it sounded wonderful. Later I came out with another woman with whom I spent the next two years.

The first concerns of an oppressed minority artist are to make identity statements loudly and clearly. If you are black, if you are gay, if you are physically challenged, you need to make those images for yourself and for the community. Once that is established and you've said, "I'm a lesbian," over and over, or you've said, "I'm black," over and over, you free yourself for other concerns. My later work has turned to more abstract cinema, cinema that's more about perception rather than representation.

I have found that the audiences who go to experimental film screenings are unfamiliar with the concerns of lesbian representation in film. Conversely, lesbian audiences know little about experimental cinema. In an effort to educate both audiences I talk and write about both experimental film and lesbian representation.

I'd like to contribute a series of films that represent one lesbian woman's life, a life lived as an artist. If historians wanted, they could go back and see the social culture that I've moved through and how my work has been influenced by the historical context. If I am honest and true to myself, the images in my films will depict a sociological representation of a lesbian in the '70s, '80s and '90s.

Happiness, for me, is having an open door with many possibilities. I try for everything which might serve to further my work. When I decide on a project, I commit myself to developing it. This commitment enriches the depth and scope of the work.

I think teaching experimental film in an elementary school would offer more possibilities to children living in a media–illiterate society. Broadcast television is pat and predictable. It's as pat as *The Readers' Digest* in a format which offers little challenge. This generation and future generations will remain passive recipients of predigested and regurgitated media pablum. We must introduce more possibilities and multiple ways of reading text and moving images.

Adults assume that children are too young to understand experimental film. However, I have shown my films to third grade classes, videotaped the childrens' responses, and turned the camera over to the children. These eight-year-olds could read the films and loved their participation in both interpretation and production. This illustrates my strong belief that we must not neglect the arts and creative expression in our schools.

Experimental film provides many more levels of expression than a linear, one-dimensional narrative cinema. I am lucky to be a filmmaker in a time when women, gays, and people of color are expanding the dimensions of what film can be. I follow a long history of women in film from Alice Guy Blaché in 1897, Leontine Sagan in the '30s, Maya Deren in the '40s, Marie Mencken in the '50s, and Gunvor Nelson in the '60s. I started making films in the late '60s and found there is still room on that big rectangle of a screen for new points of view, new gender constructions.

Success means to me that my work would reach an international audience including Asia, the Middle East, and Africa. My films would be transmitted through satellite television into peoples' homes so that I would be able to communicate to the largest number of people possible. ∎

In my forties I laid the foundation for the rest of my life, and that took persistence and determination. It is something else to be thinking, to be making art and relationship without old baggage.

—Betsy Damon

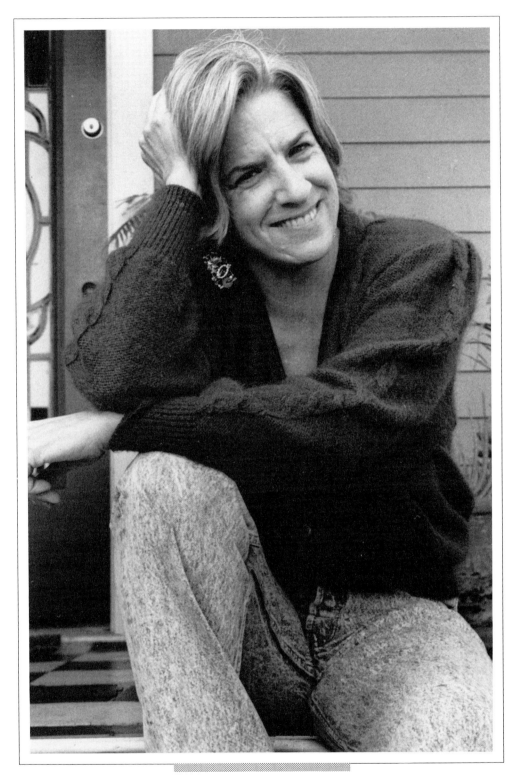

Betsy Damon

▪ P R O F I L E ▪

A long-term friend calls artist Betsy Damon a mustang. It's an interesting and accurate depiction of a woman who has a strong, energetic physical presence, and one who is feisty—ready to take on the world. And in her way she does.

In the mid-1980s Betsy developed a national network for women artists called "No Limits." Her dream is to develop a process for women through which they can eliminate the effects of sexism and discover the full extent of both their personal and artistic abilities. She feels that believing in and supporting yourself directly corresponds to believing in supporting other women to "go all the way."

Betsy thinks that one of the most pervasive effects of sexism is that it makes it difficult for women to have confidence in their own ideas, because at a very young age many females were given the message that their ideas weren't powerful or interesting enough—certainly not worth devoting their lives to. Fully aware of this condition, Betsy stubbornly maintains that we are fortunate to have been born female and that our emotional life is important, a strength. The ability to feel, to be loving, caring and nurturing in no way diminishes our capacity to think; in fact, it enhances it.

There is no question as to Betsy's staunch feminist perspective. However, she is not a separatist. Her goal is to empower everyone—women, children and men, all races and religions. Seven years and thirty five on-going support groups later her mission seems possible.

Recently Betsy has undertaken a two-year-long "Water Project" in Minnesota for which she is the community organizer—probing, educating, and unifying people's concerns about their most basic of needs: the water they drink.

In her interview she discusses the challenges she has faced in her life while trying to have it all—career, marriage and motherhood—and how she has gone from being a solitary artist to become a catalyst for meaningful community work which has far-reaching benefits for humanity and the planet.

I have made art since I was two-and-a-half. On a profound level it was the one place where I felt I could be myself without interference. When I was ten or eleven years old I chose visual art over making music. I thought, "I can make paintings in my room by myself, but you have to perform music in front of people." It was also the one place I could fully express myself.

In 1972 I organized a huge three-week festival, with a feminist emphasis. It was the first time women artists of all kinds ever got together: conductors, composers, filmmakers, theatre people, and all the different art media. There was a three-day conference at the end. Judy Chicago did a workshop and because of this experience I started a feminist studio at Cornell later that year. I went around, talked up this idea, and got $15,000, carte blanche. Nobody knew I was a faculty wife because I acted like I was somebody.

When my kids were little, neighbors who were also mothers, just hung out with each other all day long. All you are at that time is a young mom. I wanted to work in my studio, so I asked people not to visit me between ten and four when I was busy making art. I don't know if I would do that again, it's so isolating. I remember how difficult it was to keep my confidence and a sense of my identity.

I went to New York City in the fall of 1976 and left my children with their dad. Eventually the family broke up, but the painting survived. And for a while my life as a mom went too, which was really horrible. And then I decided I was able to have my children with me. The best thing in my life is when I have people close to me. I was happy when my children were little. I always knew it wasn't the children who were creating the confusion; society's attitude towards women was what was making it so hard on me.

I worked individually and with groups. We did performances and then I did events that created community. I always drew, but I rarely exhibited my drawings. Ever since the Feminist Art Studio I've done workshops for women. That went on until '83, '84. In addition to doing the performances I made installations. They were always well received. There came a time when I realized that my career was based on people offering me things, not on my going after them. In fact I found going after work almost impossible, so I'm very grateful to the people who helped me, who saw my work and invited me places and asked me to participate.

In 1980 I went to Copenhagen to organize *The Shrine for Every Woman*. It was a place for women to share their stories. It worked out so well and was so beautiful. At that point I thought, "This is the best. It won't get any better than this." I cried when we took the shrine down and went back to New York and I went about my life. I later did another shrine in Nairobi.

In 1985 my work took a new direction when I received my first big grant from the Danforth Museum. My idea was to cast 200 feet of a river bed in handmade paper. I did a meditation for the survival of the planet in the library in Albuquerque, New Mexico for eighty people and it was fantastic as far as it went, but I wanted to understand how I could get those people to *do* something, to take the next step to work for the environment.

That summer I went to a farm with my children to heal my kidneys. I began to work with stones and I thought, "Everybody picks up stones, and they think stones are magic. Why don't I do a piece called *Bring a Stone?*" I started reading anthropological texts about the Native Americans' use of stones and stones as healing. I did my first *Bring a Stone* piece and then later changed the name to *Meditations with Stones for the Survival of the Planet*.

During that time I took my children on a seven-week camping trip around the U.S. I saw many river beds in the Southwest which had become dry due to the building of dams and I got the idea of casting a dry river bed. I began researching the water in the area: what was in the water, what was happening to it? The water was undrinkable, laced with radiation and agricultural waste. I realized that this was happening everywhere in the United States. And lo and behold, it was front page news two years later. I decided that I was going to learn everything I could about water. It felt like going back to school.

I didn't care that much about making *art*; I cared about exposing environmental problems. I showed the river bed in museums and schools and began to imagine other pieces about water. People said, "Well, cast another river bed." But I really didn't want to do that. Why cast another river bed? To perfect my technique? For five years I struggled with my next idea.

I read the life of every famous woman artist that I could and tried to understand how they accomplished their lives. How did they survive? I found out that many of them spent time in mental institutions or experienced extremely stressful times. It was heartbreaking. I didn't want life to be like that for women forever.

In 1985 I started "No Limits," a workshop for women artists. I saw how women denied their own intelligence. At first, I used guided meditations, but then decided to work more directly. "No Limits" asks women to listen to each other, to take themselves and their work seriously: how to get out of the bedroom and into a studio. I too have to struggle to take myself seriously. I have to ask myself, "How serious are you about cleaning up the waters, Betsy? How far will I take my ideas? What form will they take? Am I serious in my commitment to other women?" The decision to continue leading the groups year after year was a big deal for me. It's been seven years now. I made a decision not to advertise and encouraged people to build their own networks based on their relationships and friends. The type of person who chooses to do "No Limits" is someone who's willing to go through uncomfortable feelings. And I've kept the price down so that people could really afford it.

My biggest vision is for every woman to realize her greatest dreams and not to accept limits on what she can do. "No Limits" takes on class, race, religion. It's all part of us. Whatever the issues are, we're taking them apart. "No Limits" was created from my desire to build a support group around me and find a safe way for me to proceed out into the world. That was my personal need. "No Limits" keeps me totally alert. I try not to accept any of the limitations that society says are out there. And it's everywhere. There's nothing I love more than watching other human beings go for it. When I forget about going for it myself, I watch someone else out there and they remind me. That's how it works, back and forth. Often I see women changing their lives . . . right before my eyes. All we need to do is to remind each other constantly because the forces of repression are very strong. They're both obvious and subtle, and it's the subtle parts that are the most insidious and difficult to eliminate.

I am going to Minnesota and initiating an art piece there, and I'll be working for two years on increasing water consciousness there. It is called, *Keepers of the Waters: Citizens Rights and Responsibilities*. The vision behind this piece is to bring artists together with citizens and organizations (scientific, ecological, governmental) that are dealing with water issues. Our goal is to use art as the primary form of information, inspiration, and education to create sufficient water consciousness in specific communities so that the rapid deterioration of water can be effectively changed.

Both my parents are hardcore New Englanders—Boston, New Englanders. Harvard, Vassar. They are very committed to that tradition. Being a lesbian for ten years propelled me into another life. It was great, empowering, and difficult. Then I realized I wanted to have men in my life, so I changed my life again. And that was really hard, because people had grown to identify me in a certain way. I wanted my friends to stay my friends, supporting me and enjoying the fact that I was changing my life. Only a very few people could do that, could actually enjoy the fact that I was messing with my identity. And yet, why shouldn't we do everything, have every identity we ever wanted? Why would we stay in one art form our entire lives?

My forties were perhaps the toughest times, because I began to wake up in a real sense. To do that I had to go through some very unpleasant feelings. I had to relive hurtful situations from my childhood that were so bad I had forgotten them. I had to notice that much of my life was not the way I wanted it to be and I had to change it deliberately. I don't know if this is a particularly forties' experience. I think people do that whenever they are able, and I was lucky to be able to do it in my forties. At this time I began to take myself more seriously and notice how much fear controlled my entire life. I began to live my life my way. I finally feel free to be myself more often than not, and that means that I will be able to do so much more. In my forties I laid the foundation for the rest of my life and that took persistence and determination. It is something else—to be thinking, to be making art and relationships without old baggage. ■

Going into real estate was my way of leaving home. I'd go out early in the morning, and sometimes wouldn't return until late at night. My husband took over the running of the household. It was a form of liberation. I liked being out of the house and being with adults. And I liked being an authority on something.

—Judy Phillips

Judy Phillips

▪ P R O F I L E ▪

In this time of rootlessness—one of the most pervasive and least publicized problems of modern life during the second half of the 20th century—Judy Phillips carries the awareness of the sacredness of the trinity—family, home, community—in her heart throughout her working day. A real estate broker, she feels that this is a natural profession for women, because "It is what women know best—their homes."

As a society we are inundated with the modern epidemic of "broken-homes" and the collapse of community life. There is almost an innocence, an ingenuousness, in Judy's steadfast, stalwart belief in the need to preserve the basic human values of the home, the family and the community.

She became a real estate broker around the time she turned forty, forging a successful profession for herself which eventually became a cooperative partnership with several other brokers, including her sister, Barbara Schatan. Today Judy is a member of a nonprofit organization that is dedicated to providing low-cost housing through limited equity co-op shares. A strong and resolute social consciousness propels her to share her experience and goodwill with other community members.

Family life is Judy's mainstay, and during our interview she disclosed how the recent illness of her father has put pressure on each member of her extended family, while simultaneously bringing them closer together. His illness has also given her a heightened awareness of her own mortality, as well as pointing out the importance of maintaining her physical and mental well-being and living in the moment.

Having a supportive marriage has allowed Judy to be nurturing in her friendships and secure in her work. She feels, in fact, that she is a midwife of sorts when she places people in homes where they will be happy, and then helps them settle comfortably into community life.

During our discussion I was affected by the fact that Judy repeatedly described herself as "lucky," "fortunate," or "blessed," and I realized that as a result of her positive attitude she sincerely believes that life—along with its myriad of experiences—is a gift. And living that wisdom makes *her* a gift to her family, friends, and community.

JUDY PHILLIPS

I'm quite pleased with the way that my life is going. I like to think that I have a clear path ahead, that I can keep evolving and changing and doing the things that I want to do. It's wonderful to be in my forties in this era, because there are more opportunities for women to keep moving ahead.

My work as a real estate broker is a more encompassing profession than I ever would have imagined, and that is really what has kept me in it. Being a realtor is fascinating to me. Real estate is one of the few professions that has been open to women. As long as a woman is eighteen years old, hasn't been a felon, and passes a test after taking a few classes, she can become an agent. It's wide open. That's what I like about it. Commercial real estate is dominated by men, but residential real estate is dominated by women. It deals with something that we as women know: we know our homes. In my earlier years I was searching around and wondering if I would ever find a career that suited me or that I liked. Residential real estate is a field that I felt comfortable in, challenged by, and was successful at almost right from the beginning.

I feel honored to be in this position. Once I have a connection with someone and we make the decision to work together—I get to be part of one of the most life-changing or life-enhancing events in most people's lives.

It started for me when I was in my twenties—my husband and I were lucky enough to buy (with the help of an aunt) our first home in Berkeley. That was such a high point for me—to have the security and the luxury of our own little plot of land with which we could do whatever we wanted. It made me feel like a very rich person. It grounded me in the community. While we were in Berkeley we started one of the first food conspiracies in the U.S. and joined the Neighborhood Watch and a coop nursery school. We became involved because we felt that we had a stake in the community.

Now that I'm in the profession of helping people buy their own homes, I sometimes feel like a midwife delivering the goods. I become an intimate part of people's lives and they share their stories with me. Usually they are going through a life transition: marriage, divorce, inheritance, birth, death.

I work with many single people, particularly single women buying their own homes. Single people buying their own homes is a new phenomenon in the last ten or fifteen years. I worked with two women clients who, when they bought their home twenty years ago, had serious obstacles getting a loan and title insurance because the male-dominated institutions had never seen a single woman buying property.

I naturally tend to bring people together. I enjoy networking and turning my friends on to each other, and turning people on to things. I'm gambling on my ability to bring something together for the people I'm working with. Also on some level, I am making the choice to work with people who will eventually pay off. I may invest three months, six months, a year, sometimes more in a client, and I don't get paid until the deal closes.

I grew up in a small California beach town and come from a Russian-Jewish family of merchants. My father had a shoe store, in which I worked; my grandfather had a second-hand store in downtown Los Angeles. I was brought up with someone always buying or selling something. I was raised around people gambling, playing poker, gin rummy—many compulsive gamblers. I remember large family groups under big striped umbrellas at the beach with card games going on; and when I went to sleep at night I could hear the sound of cards flapping on the tables. People strongly believed in luck. And I've often had the feeling that there is a strain of that belief in the real estate business.

My adolescence was a difficult time for me. I didn't want to leave childhood. I started menstruating at ten. By the time I was twelve I had a full woman's figure . . . and I hated it. I felt ashamed. There was no support from the culture, no initiation into womanhood. I now feel strongly about the need for rites of passage throughout our lives. This is something that the women's spirituality movement has helped me to understand and use in my life.

I felt completely lost and alienated, ashamed of my body and who I was. I stopped using my body physically and consequently began to gain weight. My life was so miserable in high school that I tried to escape by dreaming about how great it would be when I was in college. But then college came and it wasn't any better. During that period I was extremely unhappy and unstable—I had three car accidents in a row, flunked out of college, finally ran away. I didn't feel that my life began until I met Dan when I was twenty one. I welcomed him as a companion on the road of life—because I was lost, and he was too. He had also experienced disillusionment and we were two lost souls who found each other. A funny way to begin a marriage!

Both of us had come out of unhappy adolescent periods, and we had a great deal of anger that we didn't even know about. That was a big challenge in our years together— first to recognize the anger, and then to deal with it, because it would come bubbling up and out in temper tantrums and stormings out of the house. I remember when we lived in Berkeley, my brother Gary who lived down the street would say, "I walked by the house today and before I knocked I waited to see if it was shaking, or what sounds were coming out of it." We were raising our two daughters, Arianne and Caitlin, in the midst of this chaos, feeling ashamed, wanting to be "The Partridge Family"—and knowing we weren't. Eventually we went to some anger workshops and got into therapy.

Up through my twenties and into my thirties I was devoted to being a wife and mother. Then when I turned thirty, I experienced a crisis—I had to do something that was just for me. That's when I joined a writers' group. Writing became my meditation and an important part of my growth as an individual. We sold our house, left Berkeley, and bought an old resort up on the Russian River in Northern California. We went into the business of renting out twelve houses on this resort we called "Chalupka Country Cottages." The word chalupka is a Yiddish word meaning "broken down shack in the country." We formed a business partnership. We divided up the responsibilities: he did all the maintenance (he'd never hung a picture before!), and I did the management.

The four or five years that we had that resort taught me how to set limits for myself and other people. We were living with eleven households of tenants. We had a social, do-good attitude. During the first year we were ready to sell it and get out. It was one huge nightmare because I didn't know how to say no to people. I learned. We had a large piece of real estate and we supported ourselves, marginally, but we did support ourselves. And we became further involved in the community. We started a summer recreation program and a health center. It was a wonderful time in our lives when I felt that our livelihood, the place we lived, the community, our children, everything, were integrated.

There came a point where I felt that I wanted to do something that was separate from and outside of the family. I wanted to have my own career, and I wanted to prove myself in the world. So we left the Russian River and moved to Santa Cruz, where I studied for my realtor's license. I didn't have a degree in anything—I hadn't finished college. In real estate, I thought I could do well and make money, and I could be my own boss.

The first day that I was actually on the job, I remember I confused it a little with working in a shoe store. I honestly thought that you just sit there behind the desk, someone walks in and says, "Show me your wares," we would try on a few houses, one would fit like a pair of shoes, we'd wrap it up, and out the door they'd go. I had no idea that it was really a kind of magical mystery tour. I found out that often what people said they wanted and what they ended up with were two different things.

I have enjoyed my forties, experimenting with ways to have a balanced, full life. When I first started in my career, it was a way of getting out of the house. During the first year or two I became a workaholic. I used and abused the job, but at the same time I was gathering as much experience as I could, like an internship.

Going into real estate was my way of leaving home. I'd go out early in the morning, and sometimes wouldn't return until late at night. We switched roles. My husband took over the running of the household. He continued to write, teach, and play music. The kids, by that time, were ten and fifteen. It felt great. I liked being out of the house and being with adults. And I liked being an authority on something. After the initial absorption in my work, I realized that I couldn't live a life where I was working all the time; it didn't feel real to me. So I started to integrate my life more. I feel like a juggler or a tightrope walker, just keeping things in balance, because that is when I feel at my best.

These days I spend quite a bit of time with my family, and when I say family, I mean a large, extended family. I live in the same town with my two sisters, my mother, my father (who has been ill), and my ninety two-year-old grandmother. I live, virtually, within walking distance of all of them, which is a phenomenon because for twenty-five years I didn't live near my family, and now we're all in the same town.

Perhaps the most significant thing I've learned through my career is that life is a continually moving, ongoing process. And I've also learned that my ability to be successful is intertwined with my level of self-esteem and self-confidence. If I am not feeling good about myself there is no way I can relate to clients and help them to make important decisions about a house. The first thing I do with a client, before we even look at property, is to sit down and talk. I get people to tell me their fantasies about their ideal home. I help people materialize their fantasy. Sometimes what they end up with is very different from the original fantasy. One of the things I do when I show a piece of property, especially if it isn't what the client originally had in mind, is visualize what it would be like if they were living there. You can take the same property and put a hundred different people in it, and every single person, from the moment they walk in the door and put a cup down on a table, transform it according to who they are. So I use my imagination and try to get people to open up their imaginations. I also have a practical sense about money and I help people to translate the figures down into what they can actually afford. And sometimes, even if they can't afford it, through brainstorming we can figure out ways how, through alliances with other people, or with help from their family, they can get into a piece of property.

About seven years ago through the influence of my friends, I became aware of the women's spirituality movement. I started doing some workshops and in my mid-forties went to my first Women's Alliance Solstice Camp. The experience has opened me up, and every year I go back and rediscover another little part of myself, another part of the whole that hasn't been fully explored. I look forward to it as a time of rejuvenation.

I'm fortunate to have such a great role model for aging as my grandmother, Magrew. Magrew is ninety-two years old, and lives here in Santa Cruz with my mother and father. She is in excellent physical and mental condition. She reads constantly, took up the violin five years ago, and is physically active. Recently Magrew became a volunteer in the schools, giving talks about her life. She is interested in young people and what they are doing. Magrew went into real estate in her fifties and became a broker in her sixties with seven or eight people working for her. She always says I'm following in her footsteps, and I probably am. I feel lucky to have her, because she helps me to see that with good luck, good health, and a good attitude, every year of my life can be a growing year. Magrew is a steady flame in front of me.

I'm proud of my two daughters. They are now in their twenties, and are really delightful and beautiful human beings. I am blessed now to be part of their lives. I enjoyed them when they were younger, but there were times when I really wondered if it was worth it. I was afraid that I would not be close to them, but I feel that I have real allies in them.

Through staying with something long enough I've been able to work things out. There were several points along the road in my marriage where it would have been just as easy to leave it as to stay with it. One thing that has kept me going, though, was the belief that whatever I didn't work out in this one, if I left it, I'd have to work out somewhere else. I don't know if young people these days appreciate family life, because they are so busy with two careers, running here and running there. If you want to be a family you have got to spend time together. I always felt, when times got tough, that as long as the family was together then everything else would work out. ∎

When we get to be 40 or 45 years old we have a wonderful base of experience to transform ourselves. It takes incredible courage to leap off the bridge of what we've known, who we've been, and how we've defined ourselves, but there's so much richness in the water below when we jump.

—Brooke Medicine Eagle

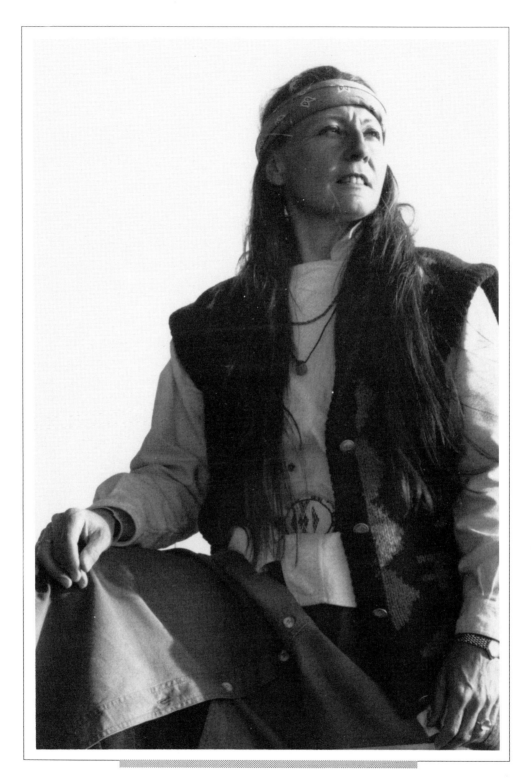

Brooke Medicine Eagle

▪ P R O F I L E ▪

Beauty before me,
Beauty behind me,
Beauty above me,
Beauty below me,
Beauty all around me,

I walk in Beauty.

—Navaho Chant

As I awaited the arrival of native American métis Brooke Medicine Eagle, I was amused by the incongruence of our meeting place—the Newark, New Jersey, International Airport. The irony of interviewing in an airport a woman who lives in Montana and is known for her love and dedication to the wilderness didn't escape me. Yet Brooke is a person who is also dedicated to sharing her Earth wisdom, and thus travels internationally for a good part of the year. So here I was—the airport being the compromise for two hectic traveling schedules. When a blue Toyota pickup truck pulled into the unloading zone and out stepped a tall, sturdy woman with brown waist-length hair held in place by a rolled bandana, wearing a long gathered skirt and cowboy boots, I knew she had arrived. After checking her luggage and securing a boarding pass, we entered the airport coffeeshop and began a professional interview which soon became a friendly conversation. Brooke's unguarded nature is refreshing and without artifice.

She laughingly calls herself a "renegade spirit," and says, "I've been a role model for many women who are struck by the fact that I live my life guided by my visions, and that it works!" Brooke Medicine Eagle is an Earthkeeper, healer, teacher, performer, and leader of celebrations, dedicated to learning from the inherent wisdom of this planet Earth we call home. She is an enrolled member of the Crow Indian tribe, yet her lineages are a rainbow of Crow, Lakota Sioux, and Nez Percé, as well as European. She is grandniece of Chief Joseph, the Nez Percé leader.

Through visions and dreams she was given her sacred name, Medicine Eagle. This name has called her to use her ability to "fly high and see far" (the way of vision and prophecy), and to carry the messages and light of a new time strongly across the sky. She asserts, "The name is not just a name like Joe or

Nancy—it is an assignment." Her focus is on global issues and her message is to teach people to live in an easy harmony with the land, much as her ancestors did. Although the native tradition was hidden when she was growing up in economically impoverished circumstances on a Crow Reservation in Montana, Medicine Eagle has spent her entire life absorbing and studying the ways of nature.

Her visions call her to be a carrier of the message of harmony between two cultures—to bring the ancient ways of knowing and being back for the new dominant culture. She feels that as human beings who are the caretakers of the planet, each of us two-leggeds have the responsibility to help bridge that gap, to build that bridge into the new age of balance.

From her Sky Lodge Ranch near the Bob Marshall Wilderness in Montana, Medicine Eagle travels eight months out of each year, balancing her continued teaching and participation in international conferences. She takes students into the wilderness to learn from those she calls "the finest teachers—Mother Earth and Father Spirit." Through training camps, ceremonies, retreats and vision quests, she invites others to experience the ancient ways which she hopes will be a source of healing for them and in turn a benefit for all beings.

Brooke's primary interest is in the renewal of ancient ritual forms of creating a beautiful path upon the Earth. Her ceremonial arts camp, Song of the Beauty Way, is described as, "turning our attention to the creation and sustaining of beauty in the exquisite garden of Mother Earth." She touches the lives of many women who come to her for guidance. As each one of them is transformed, she shines the light of that inner attainment and makes a positive difference in the world.

One of the interesting things about my life as I've looked back over it, in comparison to other people of my age, is that I was raised by the standards of the 1800s and yet walk the edge of an awakening consciousness in the 1990s. During my childhood we lived in the wilderness five miles from the nearest ranch, ten miles from the little village, and seventy five miles from a major town. My family didn't have much money so we did everything ourselves. Whether it was veterinary procedures, carpentry, making fences, herding cattle on horseback, or any part of ranching, I participated. My brother and I would ride our ponies all over the prairies and canyons near our home ranch. I remember the beauty of spring-fed streams running through quaking aspen groves filled with deer. I remember eating sweet wild currants, chokecherries and plums.

The reservation schools then were very poor. I guess they met the government standards for having somebody in front of a classroom, but that was about it. My mother understood that education would make a difference for us kids. She saw that so many young women by the time they were sixteen or seventeen were pregnant, or had one or two kids, or were alcoholic. She wanted us to leave that environment and get an education.

Having no resources for a college education, I applied for scholarships at many schools. One day I had the wonderful good fortune—I feel that Spirit has been with me throughout my life—of going to the mailbox and finding a large envelope with gold lettering from a place called the University of Denver in Colorado. I hadn't applied. I'd never even heard of it before! I opened it up and the letter said, "We invite you to come to the University of Denver on a Centennial Scholarship, which means you will have full room and board and full tuition for four years." I said, "You've enrolled yourself an Indian kid!" When I headed for college I had fifty dollars in my pocket.

I received a marvelous education there majoring in psychology and mathematics, and graduating Phi Beta Kappa. Because of my profound interest in healing, I had thoughts of becoming a doctor or nurse, yet I shifted to the study of psychology, because I was fascinated to learn more about people and how they function. These studies eventually brought me into contact with many alternative types of healing, including those practiced by native peoples throughout the world. I am grateful for having gained a perspective which is broader and deeper than that of the established medical field; much power for healing lies within that perspective.

I lived in northern California at the time of the incredible awakening of consciousness and the early human potential movement, and my life expanded tremendously. I began to see the enormous richness of my life, which I had not realized until I lived around people with much more conventional backgrounds, many of whom were financially wealthy compared to my impoverished childhood. I realized how abundant my environment had been with possibility and inventiveness and resourcefulness. It was wonderful in those ways, yet our family was really dysfunctional. It was sometimes very lonely, and when there was difficulty within the family, I turned to the wilderness, to the trees and the animals. I would go and lie on the hillsides and be healed. Thus, I developed a depth of connection with Mother Earth that I might not have if my situation had been more pleasant.

Before I started teaching, my guides and elders said, "Well, you're a teacher, of course." And I asked, "A teacher of what?" Then I began to look at other people's experiences, and to realize that they didn't have any connection with the earth. *That* was my gift. To find what one has to offer others is a mysterious search, because the most profound gift one has seems ordinary—yet it is of primary importance in living a creative and expressive life.

I've written a book called *Buffalo Woman Comes Singing*. It's a chronicle of my life, framed in teaching stories as metaphors for other people. Many of the issues I've faced in my life and worked with in my spirit are exactly the things I see in my students. I may have taken a few steps more and may therefore have an elder sister's guidance and encouragement, but my life is not that different. People need to find guidance within themselves for opening their hearts to a much larger experience of life. I hope the stories in the book will teach and support and encourage people on their paths.

The name "Medicine Eagle" was given to me in a vision at a traditional fasting and questing site of the Cheyenne and Lakota people on Bear Butte in South Dakota. I was given the very long name "Daughter of the Rainbow of the Morning Star Clan, Whose Helpers Are the Sun and the Moon, and Whose Medicine is the Eagle"; it soon shortened to Medicine Eagle. That vision (spoken of at length in *Buffalo Woman Comes Singing*) was quite extraordinary for me in many ways. I was coming out of an academic setting and had been very left-brained. This important spiritual experience opened up a whole new consciousness of my feminine, creative, artistic side. It also gave me a strong direction for my work in the world, some of which involved working with women's mysteries and the spiritual use of our moon (menstrual) time to serve the larger life around us with a different kind of feminine creativity. That process of going into the "womb of creation" through retreat and deep listening has continued to be a guiding force in my life.

I've always had an interest in greater humanity—a global view of things—and what it means to be human. I am less interested in what it means to be a Crow Indian or a student in San Francisco or a business woman in New York, than I am in the question of how each of us two-leggeds can live a truly human life. Through not only Native American elders, but also through other important teachers like the Israeli genius, Moshé Feldenkrais, I have continued to look for answers about who we are as human beings. The *Rainbow Medicine Way* in which I am interested carries a vision of global consciousness, a call to look at the entire rainbow of life: white, black, red and yellow—all children of Mother Earth and Father Spirit in every color, dimension, and level of life. All have to be respectfully taken into account.

Even though I have had a great number of powerful and positive teachers, I have also gained much from disappointments in my learning process. In several instances when I went to very traditional medicine women for training, I was heartbroken to discover that though they know the old forms—they know how to paint my face, and to pray in a traditional way—I found little in their hearts which had to do with Spirit or goodness, loving or caring. As much as it disappointed me, there was much wisdom to be gained. Those experiences helped me to understand that the important thing is not the face paint, the beads, and feathers. It isn't about the forms, traditional or otherwise; it's about the Spirit that lives within everything. To touch that place of Spirit has been my quest, and I think it is a powerful quest for all human beings. One of the ways we can get to that place is through exploring the ancient truths. Native philosophies have held these truths most clearly for people of this time. I believe that these truths comes through every tradition when that tradition is pure. So rather than the outward form, I've sought the inner essence. I was once told, "You will never have a traditional form. The process you follow will break through form into Spirit."

We need to change ourselves deep inside, change our hearts and the way we've connected to all of life, change our consciousness and awaken our spirit in order to have life on earth continue. Sacred ecology is the harmonious way of living that involves the Spirit and the aliveness found in everything. Spirit lives in all creatures, not only in human beings. The earth is conscious and our relationship with her can bring about a beautiful and creative way of life that's harmonious and peaceful rather than damaging and disrespectful.

I feel the tenuousness of our present human position. I believe that the AIDS epidemic is also a statement about Mother Earth, who is herself dangerously close to slipping into a fatal condition. If we don't begin to take care of Mother Earth, I think she will reach the point where she is unable to fight back and be healthy. We're very near that point, and when it shifts, it will shift very fast. I'm alarmed, to say the least, by where we've come and by how little consciousness there is about this state of emergency.

There is a sense of urgency in my own experience and in my teaching that says we need to move rapidly and make enormous changes now in order to make a difference.

There is hope if people will begin to awaken that spiritual part of themselves—that heartfelt acknowledgment that we are the caretakers of life on this planet. The people who especially need that inner experience are those who are in command and control, those who can make the difference. I'm interested in working with people such as corporate presidents and government officials who touch the lives of the masses. I love what Jimmy Carter is doing with his life. He's out there building and working at whatever level he thinks he can, making a difference in people's lives at a grassroots level.

I'm a "workaholic" in the sense that my life revolves around my work. For many years I thought I had a personal life, but when I began to mature I realized that I didn't. I wasn't doing anything I really wanted to do. I lived on the road in my car for twelve years, and suddenly realized that I didn't know myself as a person separate from the work I do and the tremendous drive I have to facilitate change in the world. Yet that's shifting in my life now. I've had a home in Montana for five years and I'm examining family issues. Of course family, intimacy and community are the hardest part for me: because as a child I had such poor examples of them. There are some new wrinkles in these old eyes that come from having recently faced the fact that there's a personal piece missing in my life. *And*, it's exciting to be dealing with these issues, and to see new patterns emerging through that attention! My family and my home in the wilderness are a source of joy and solidity for me these days.

I've chosen not to have children for many reasons. A primary one is my commitment to my work, but others are important as well. Not having an extended family or community in which to raise children made it less than attractive; also, I did not like to think of giving a young, wise being over to the current school system for years of indoctrination in an old, outmoded way of life and learning. Now my visions are guiding me to interact more with children. Although I'm presently on the road many months a year, perhaps at some time I'll have a settled environment where I can have young people in my home. I'd like to have children around me, perhaps adopt one of the children in need of a caring family, yet I don't have any sense that I'll have my own child. But who can be sure until moon-pause (menopause) makes that official.

Right now I'm moving toward realizing my artist self. After years of thinking of myself as very non-artistic, I have come to understand that I am presently an artist at many levels of my life. Making actual objects of beauty and statements of importance is something I will do more of as years go by. I've often said that I spent the first thirty years of life figuring out my childhood; the next thirty I'll be spending as a teacher on the road; and another thirty I'll spend as a fine artist. I used to add to that teasingly, "In my fourth thirty years, I'll be the madam of a whorehouse," just to shock everyone. But I do think I will live to be very, very old.

I'm offering many camps in the wilderness of Montana for women, including one called Song of Beauty Way. The camp is devoted to learning to walk a beautiful path and create beauty in the world, through the metaphor of ritual art and craft. We do beading and leatherwork, make baskets and rattles—wonderful ceremonial objects. I bring in the finest beading teachers in the area and then I get to sit down and bead myself. This kind of thing begins to connect my work teaching other women to my new self as an artist.

Since I turned forty I've been awakening to a greater sense of myself, one that includes both my developing talents and my personal issues. A saying of my teacher Moshé Feldenkrais has come back to me a lot: "You can't give away something you don't have." Several years ago, I began turning my attention toward teaching peace and harmony for all peoples. Yet I looked inside myself and realized that I didn't have these qualities fully developed within myself. I encouraged others to be in harmony with the land, and yet I was on the road so much I didn't know the plants that lived in the meadows and forest around my own home. So I'm working on living the kind of existence where my life is a model at deeper and deeper levels.

I think the middle years are a wonderful opportunity for women to take some time off and see if they've yet figured out who they are. It could be retreating somewhere for two weeks in a little cabin and not seeing another person, or anything that allows them to get away from who they think they are and what has defined them. And then, with a warrior's courage, to go for becoming who they truly are. We came into this life to give certain gifts, and if we don't give them no one else ever will. We are so unique, so individual; it would be a precious gift lost to the world if we don't share ourselves fully. The gifts we contribute from that kind of warrior stance will be much more profound than the gifts we give by living as society prescribes.

There is such knowledge and experience, power and beauty in women as they grow older. There's a kind of freeing up: we feel less concerned about how we look or what other people think. We've entered a powerful time in our lives, where we have great wisdom.

It's important to start paying attention to ourselves, to be healthy and vital, because without that physical body foundation we don't have the stamina to be who we really are and to give what we have to offer. When we get to be forty or forty five years old we have a wonderful base of experience to transform ourselves. Everything we've done, whether it was raising children or working at jobs or traveling around the world, gives us what we need for the next step. We haven't wasted any time. It takes incredible courage to leap off the bridge of what we've known, who we've been and how we've defined ourselves, but there's such richness in the waters below when we jump. I would encourage women to really go for it in their lives.

Lately I've had an interesting thought: what if each stage of our development is just school for the next step? What will be the next adventure? What will I be graduating to? There's a wealth of learning continually happening. It's so exciting! I really have the sense of myself at sixty years old of having an entirely different life. And then again at ninety having a birth into another kind of life that's very powerful. This is an exciting time in a woman's life. Very, very much so. ∎

Women begin to hit their stride in their forties, because often they've spent their early years juggling so many different activities that they were simply making it through the day. But then they reach a point where they are able to integrate their life experiences.

—Cokie Roberts

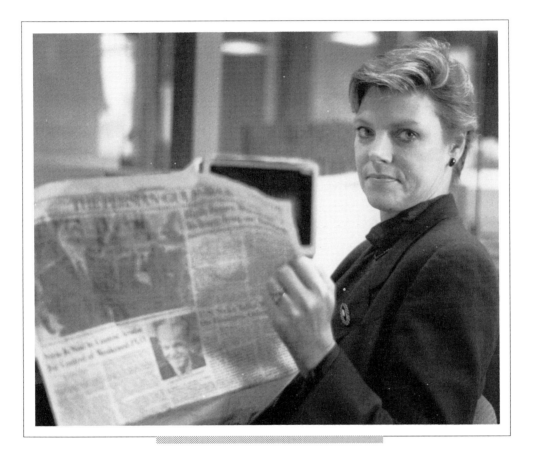

Cokie Roberts

Riding the Amtrac Metropolitan line at 6:03 on a wet, 35° Thursday (still dark and dismal) morning from Penn Station to the recently refurbished and surprisingly grand Union Station in Washington, D.C., I prepared myself for a meeting with Cokie Roberts, a special correspondent for ABC News and a political analyst for National Public Radio. Nicknamed Cokie, because her brother Robert couldn't pronounce Corinne, her name has become one recognized by millions of listeners of *Morning Edition* on NPR as well as by the devoted viewers of *This Week With David Brinkley*, on Sunday mornings on ABC.

This was my first visit to the Capitol building on Pennsylvania Avenue where I was to rendezvous with the Congressional correspondent, Cokie Roberts. Nothing could have prepared me for the dignity and grandeur that I found in that stately building. It is easy to see why she "loves working in the Capitol building—the smallest town in America." Filled with art and permeated with American history, it gives the onlooker a sense of history and an aesthetic satisfaction. We were to meet in the Senate TV/radio gallery where journalists and news broadcasters observe Congress in action.

I walked down a dimly-lit hall with dark, cell-like offices. The only apparent source of light seemed to come from the glow of the monitors televising the proceedings in the Senate gallery. I was met by an attractive woman, tall and imposing, her blond hair clipped conveniently short, her confident demeanor echoing her Ivy League (Wellesley) education. Cokie Roberts is obviously at ease with herself and, I imagine, with any situation. The source of that assurance is easy to trace back to a childhood spent divided between New Orleans and Washington, D.C. where her father, Hale Boggs, was a Congressman. After his death in 1972, Roberts' mother, Lindy Boggs, was elected to her husband's House seat which she held until 1990 when she retired from office in order to care for her ailing daughter Barbara Boggs Sigmund (a former mayor of Princeton, New Jersey). Since childhood her mother has remained friend and confidante to Cokie as well as one of her primary influences. Only the night before our meeting, she had attended the surprise seventy-fifth birthday party for her mother in New Orleans.

She led me to an impersonal, windowless compartment where we sat for forty-five claustrophobic minutes. She spoke in a clear, deliberate voice that invited give and take. Occasionally the journalist got the better of her and she unexpectedly popped out with: "So what about you? . . ." She seemed genuinely concerned about underprivileged women and children in America and had strong feelings about the nation's crisis in health care and education. She spoke with conviction and authority and it was evident why she is considered one of the top women journalists today.

I was married young and had children early. I didn't make that decision—it was just what one did at that time. And for me it was certainly the right thing to do. Compared with people I see struggling to make the decision whether or not to have children, I found it so much easier to just go ahead and do it. The main message I try to get across to young women is that they have lots of opportunities to say no to jobs and still be able to have a good career at a later time. They don't have to say yes to a good job if it comes along when it's the wrong time in their family's life. I'm sure there are jobs along the way in my life that might have been interesting, but the decision to put my family concerns first was absolutely the right thing to do. Because I had my children young, the pressures of child-rearing are finished and I now have two delightful human beings who are fun and totally charming to be around.

My workday begins in the early morning on the radio. I get up around six, go out and get the papers—*The Washington Post*, *The New York Times* and *The Wall Street Journal*—to make sure nothing has happened on whatever issue I'm about to discuss on the program. I go on the air at 7:00 a.m. The studio was kind enough to install a line directly into my house. It's wonderful—I can broadcast from home in my nightgown! One day when my dog was overheard barking on the air it revealed all my secrets!

By 10:00 or 10:30 a.m. I normally arrive at the Capitol Building. This afternoon I'm conducting a series of interviews on arms sales for a piece I'm trying to get on the air tomorrow morning. Then I either sit down and write the program that will air the next morning or hold the material until I can write it, because something like this can't be done live; it's got to be edited. I either go on the air that night, or I'm doing interviews that I put into a piece the next day.

My husband and I don't do the Washington social scene. Since we are both in the comfortable position of working for national news organizations, we don't need to meet someone at a cocktail party in order to have access to them. And when our children were young we'd go directly home after work to be with them. Once we got into that pattern we realized we liked that better. It's much more pleasant to get home.

I have never been really interested in career success. What I do is vaporous. It literally goes out over the air and disappears. So I don't have any illusions that it's some lasting work. However, it matters to me to do a job well. In my profession there is so much of yourself in the job, you can't hide who you are—it's your voice, your face, your words, all of that—so it's important to do it well. I think success is being a whole person. The fact that I have a family—not just my own kids, but relationships with my extended family, which is intact and has remained loving and fun—is by far the most important element in my life.

To think that women try to be just like men is sad. It's significant for young women to understand they have a special role in this world. The main thing I've learned is the necessity for women to be caretakers of the children, of the elderly, of education, of health care, of the culture. Even though women have always held the role of caretaker, I worry that as they take on other functions they will lose the role that they *must* play. That would be terrible.

It's necessary for young women to remember that most of them will live a very long life. The longevity of our species just keeps increasing. The time between school and death is likely to be sixty or seventy years. So there is time; they don't have to do everything in the first five years. My advice to women would be to take some time and do whatever it is they think is of value: it might be traveling the world, or writing a book, or going into the Peace Corps. Or, on the other hand, they can start a family young, as I did, and say no to job opportunities until their children are older, because there's still plenty of years ahead for a career. There's no need to succeed instantly. You can wear out very young that way.

I think it would be boring not to be able to do a variety of different jobs somewhere along the way. Fortunately, I was on a much less direct track because I was traveling the world with my husband who was a correspondent for *The New York Times*. I did some television production, some writing, some radio—it was much more interesting than just coming out of college and going to work in television and doing that for the next thirty years.

Women journalists in my generation broke down most of the barriers, but there were a few who came before us—people like Pauline Frederick and Marleen Saunders who were really all alone in the field and did a tremendous amount to open up doors for the rest of us. Barbara Walters and Nancy Dickerson were also alone for a long time and made a big difference for women coming up after them.

The tragedy of my forties has been that my sister died of cancer at the age of fifty-one, a year after she was diagnosed. She tried desperately to make it easy for everyone, but it was a terrible experience for us. Your forties are usually the time when you begin to understand your own mortality. It is something that matures you quite dramatically. And as a result of my sister's illness, my mother, who worked in this very building, decided to retire in order to be with my sister in New Orleans. That's also been quite difficult for me, because I loved having my mother here.

Part of my fantasy of aging has been destroyed by my sister's death, because it never occurred to me that she wouldn't be in the rocking chair next to me. In my family there are many positive examples of people who aged gracefully. My mother is quite a beautiful, active, seventy-five-year-old. My aunts and grandmothers and all my relatives lived very long lives, had a grand time, and went out kicking. No one ever became senile. I've never had fears about aging. Quite the contrary. When I met my husband I was eighteen and I remember thinking, "When I have gray hair, this is the man I want to be sitting with on the porch, watching our grandchildren play." And that's my notion. I don't have any concept of slowing down, although I know I will be doing different things. I feel strongly that for women like me who were not able to do much volunteer work in our "productive years" it is important that we contribute our time in our later years. The community needs us.

I enormously admire women in public office, because seeing them up close, I know what a tremendous amount of work they do. They represent not only, say, the eighth district of California but also the women and children of America, because nobody else is putting those people at the top of the agenda.

Women begin to hit their stride in their forties, because often they've spent their early years juggling so many different activities that they were simply making it through the day. But then they reach a point where they are able to integrate their life experiences and do something that can make a difference. To me the notion of someone under forty being a serious analyst of national politics doesn't make sense. Under that age most people simply haven't walked on the earth long enough to be able to pull it together. It distresses me in the TV media world—of course, that's where it's most noticeable, because of the looks issue. The networks should be (and are to some degree) going in the direction of having older, more experienced people who can put the news in context and tell you what it all means. Any kid can go out and say, "Here's what happened today." That's easy. But it's *why* it happened and *what* it means that's significant, requiring the depth which comes with age.

I've liked my forties better than any other decade, but I think it takes time to get good at what you do. And when you reach that point it is very satisfying. ■

Since I've been forty I've connected very
powerfully with the world in a spiritual way.

—Deena Metzger

Deena Metzger

· P R O F I L E ·

Familiar to feminists and activists in the women's spirituality movement is a photographic portrait of a woman—arms expressively outstretched, ready to embrace the world, face upturned to the light, a human sunflower enjoying the supreme ecstasy of being alive.

One breast is unashamedly exposed, the other is more noticeable by its absence, cut off by a surgeon's scalpel. The breast, symbol of female nurturing, has become confused with sexuality in Western culture. Breast equals woman. A single breast, or no breasts, implies loss of womanhood/femaleness. The scar from this operation, however, recalls the archetypal female warrior, the Amazon, who deliberately cut off her breast to be a better warrior.

Through tattooing with the care given to an illuminated manuscript, an intricately designed branch of a tree has been permanently inscribed and sinuously makes its home from Deena's arm to heart. The sudden grip of empathy felt by every woman who views this portrait is palpable and piercing.

Deena Metzger is a woman who has lived through the dark night of the soul, survived *the descent to the goddess* and returned to reveal, like Inanna, her journey through the underworld. She is steeped in the ethos of mythology, using it not only as a learning tool, but as a living modality.

In the mundane world, one has rare opportunity to meet an original mind. Deena's is certainly such—utterly alive to the moment, ever curious and challenging to understand the true meaning behind words, both written and spoken. Her eyes dance with intelligence and genuine concern for other people's well-being, whether emotional, physical, or spiritual.

My first personal encounter with Deena Metzger came when I joined her Wednesday evening writers' group, "a witchy sort of group" as she described it. I was intrigued. The writing exercises led us into emotional labyrinths. We wrote our own eulogies. We viewed our personal foibles, failings, secret madnesses, and neurotic tendencies, sometimes through the perspective of a beloved family member, sometimes through the perspective of a friend or ex-lover. We gave our reasons for daily choosing life over death, explained what makes us get up in the morning. We wrote a novel in seven weeks. We wrote our life story as a personal and collective myth. We tried to live through the identity of another. I was hooked.

This is not only writing, but deep personal exploration, psychological unearthing, excavation of the mind, guided by one who has survived. Deena grew up in a traditional Jewish family and evolved into "a pagan Buddhist"; married and divorced; raised children; was raped; lost a professional position and, subsequently, recognition; had her dearest companions die; got a life-threatening disease. Deena Metzger is vibrant proof of the possibility of survival through personal suffering and pain. We learned by her example.

A courageous mind/heart uses such trials as grist for their own mill. For Deena Metzger, poet and novelist, they have become art. Her book *Tree* is a disturbing, yet poignantly available, firsthand account of dealing with cancer. These traumas have become the experiential foundation upon which her work as writer and teacher is built.

There are few women's issues that Deena has not personally experienced. The words spoken of Anaïs Nin (a close personal friend of Deena's for ten years before she succumbed to cancer) could easily be applied to Deena, herself: "All of her work was authentic—she lived it all." The numinous quality of their friendship seems to have provided the epiphany for a personal transformation: what Deena admired in another, she has now become herself.

One of the teachings Deena has learned is that our lives are indeed a journey and "if we recognize the signs we will understand the life." This is a woman who, during the course of her fortieth year, commanded her powers and conquered breast cancer. In the process, she became an inspirational role model for thousands of women. In *Tree* Deena described a special gift she'd received from a friend.

> ...a flower sealed perfectly in glass, a dandelion turned white, ready for wishing upon. Her card said, "At forty I wish to help you say 'yes' to the consequences of your life."
>
> So I say, "Yes," even now when I know the consequences. I have had my life more since I was forty than ever, more in the last days than ever. More every day, than ever.

At the end of a long and winding dirt road, high on a hill which overlooks Topanga Canyon, a rural community slightly north of Los Angeles, Deena lives with her 'familiar,' Timber, a half-wolf dog who possesses the penetrating eyes and presence of his ancestors. They are happy. Her Peace Pole stands solitarily in her garden, a prophetic sentinel who bespeaks a more gentle world. On it is inscribed the multi-lingual prayer: May Peace Prevail On Earth.

According to Aristotle, a person could be possessed by good demons. These he called Eudemons and their presence induced a joyous state of rational good works and an active life. Having tempered her dark demons of destruction and loss, Deena Metzger has earned the grace and blessings of eudemonia, a profound inner experience of euphoria and joy.

Probably the most important thing that's happened to me since I've been forty is that I've connected very powerfully with the world in a spiritual way. This has not diminished my political concerns, but I recognize that during the last ten years I have added the spiritual to the political. And now, at fifty, I think I'm beginning to work politically by working spiritually.

For example, ten years ago I would have gone out to the Nevada test site and demonstrated, and though I might still do that—I think people should demonstrate—I work politically with people to help them to make an *inner* change. I have a sense that connecting to the planet in a spiritual way—understanding and experiencing the actual divinity of the planet—is ultimately more efficient in making change than demonstrating. At least for me. So I'm watching my energy go in new places.

Life has definitely gotten better. It really does get better. There are things that are hard; the body thing gets hard. But, whoa! Love is better, sex is better. There's more intelligence, more heart, more warmth, much more contact with myself, deeper knowing of myself, as I get older. And I have such appreciation of the world we've been given.

But getting here has been extremely difficult; difficult since childhood. I can look back at the kind of child I was and see how different I was from my parents' expectations and, really, from everyone around me. I did not know how to value who I was or how to negotiate for her.

I was sitting here at home this winter, about one o'clock in the morning. There was a fire. I had a glass of brandy, and I thought: "She could never have imagined getting here." That little girl, the five-year-old or the eight-year-old or the twelve-year-old. She wanted to get here, but she couldn't. She would have been unable to imagine it. And I felt so moved by the life that I had managed, and rather astonished. She didn't know how to do it, and I don't know how I did it. It's a real surprise. Though there was a straight line between her and me. I could not have choreographed this development with my own intelligence.

I think it was a combination of what I did and what I was led to. We're often broken before something else can come in, and we would never choose that brokenness. We don't know at that moment if something else is going to come; it may not, of course. There are no guarantees; sometimes brokenness is just brokenness. I experienced a series of traumatic and difficult events in my life on the one hand, and also I was privileged to be accompanied by some dogged and persistent idealism from the time that I was very young. And I had wonderful friends. Wonderful companions. I think these combinations led me here.

When I was Deena Posy from Brooklyn, I grew up and did all the things that little girls are supposed to do: I became a teacher, married a doctor, had babies, began to write, was a political activist.

But I didn't know anything. I didn't know how to get a scholarship to Brandeis in order to complete my last two years; I didn't know how to leave home without getting married; I didn't know how to become a T.A. when I was attending graduate school, which, ultimately, was my great fortune. (If I had received my Ph.D., it would have completely ruined my life. I don't know what could have exploded me out from all that, but it would have had to have been very violent.) And I didn't know that when I said, "Well, you change one diaper, you change two" that it was the most stupid thing a woman could ever say. I wish I'd had kids after I knew myself as a creative person, as an established writer. Earlier, I was struggling for my own life and my own identity so fiercely. It's not a time to also be trying to raise children and nurture them. I think we all lost.

As a child and young adult, I was always hiding and also fighting for the part of me that was not at all conventional. I was always trying to find some way in which my individuality could be expressed without destroying everything. You have to know you are unhappy before you can act and that knowledge is a gift not everyone has. So many of us feel that we "should" do things. We're so caught in "ought" that we may know we are unhappy, but if we don't know that we've a right to our lives, and if we don't have a sense of a greater vision, we will perform our "duty" in many, many different ways.

So it took cancer to put me in a state of mind where I realized that I cared about whether I lived or died. I had to come to caring. I had to cut out all the voices in me that wanted to die, the unconscious voices, very subtle and punitive, that plague us. And then one day I finally said: "My teaching situation is making me sick, I'm NOT going to do it." It was an incredible gesture for freedom and for valuing myself. For wholeness. When I work with people in my therapeutic practice I say: "Let's try to find the deep grief or the place where life is being squelched. Let's try to change this before death or illness comes and kicks you in the ass."

If you look at individual illnesses and the people who have them, you will see that there is a psychological affinity between that particular illness—the particular manifestation—and the conditions of the psyche. If you can interpret that well enough and deeply enough, and if you can find the part in you which really wants to live, then you have a chance to write a different play, a different story, a different life.

I have been relentless in the exploration of my psyche and trying to be an honest woman. It's been eleven years now since I had cancer and that feels like (knock on wood) immense good luck. During and after that experience, everything changed. I completely and absolutely changed my life. I left the man I was living with. I changed my diet and, when my kids were old enough to be on their own, I moved here to Topanga. I left teaching in an institutional or academic setting forever and began working privately, teaching privately. I had no idea if I could earn a living that way. I was completely terrified, but I did it anyway.

Having cancer took me into a spiritual life. Around that time I began reading and thinking about the Goddess and all kinds of things began to happen. My writing changed. I was taken in a direction I never could have expected or predicted. I committed myself to my writing in a completely different way. I always thought I would be a writer, but felt that I was never managing it and, consequently, felt a great deal of failure from the ages of five to twenty-five. Nothing I did, it seemed to me, supported the idea that I would ever become a writer. I continued to be disappointed in whatever literary efforts I made. It was quite awful. Partly, I think, I didn't know whether it was my father's desire for me to become a writer or my own need, *my* desire.

But I told myself that I would never be a writer if I didn't write a novel by the time I was twenty-five. I don't know when I told myself that, but I did believe it. So, dutifully, at twenty-four, I sat down and wrote my first novel. It was a very difficult time for me because I had one child and was pregnant with my second child, in the middle of graduate school, and politically active.

So I got that first novel out of the way and it was terrible! Fortunately, I didn't have any judgment, because if I had stopped to evaluate it, I never would have written again. When I look back, though, there are certain stylistic aspects which are interesting. But, God, there was so much that I didn't know.

Since then my writing has always been on the edge, so the task has been to find a way to be on the edge and to be accessible at the same time. That has been my creative difficulty. I've managed it by just working and working and working until it happened. I want to use a Yiddish word which is *sitzfleisch:* sitting flesh.

I don't think I really accomplished the combination of clarity and risk until I wrote *Tree* which is useful to women, although more complicated than many books on people's personal experience with cancer. Still, that is a place in which there is direct speech from my experience to the reader.

In 1966 I was thirty years old and met Anaïs Nin who was about sixty-two. We had a friendship for ten years during which time I saw her once a month until she died. Knowing Anaïs was a great fortune in my life. Without question she had great influence on my work as a writer and my life as a woman. She was a most extraordinary and generous person.

By the time we met, Anaïs was already formed. It's very rare to meet a real person. Anaïs was a real person, a real woman. She was a fully developed human being who had great range and enormous courage. She was adventurous and unique; her life was like a fantasy that had been realized.

Anaïs and I talked about literature, creativity, dreams—about being a woman. She was very open with me as I was with her. From our interaction I understood that if I were really going to be a writer, creativity had to be applied equally to my life as to my work; I could not separate them. I had to learn to live the writer and write the life.

So many writers don't do that and you see it in their work. When I pick up a piece which may be glorious in terms of technique or its intelligence, I find there's something missing. I would rather have a piece of writing that is flawed in a literary way but has authenticity behind it, which has been tested in the writer's life. All of Anaïs' work was tested. It is all authentic. It is so hard to be conscious, to remember, to try to live an authentic life. *Everything* is against it in this culture.

Anaïs looked at my work, carried it to New York, brought it to editors, did everything she possibly could to support it. She never went to New York without someone's manuscript in her hand. So, when I say she was generous, I mean she was *really* generous. Many young women think, "Some day I will and maybe I can..." as we do when we are young. But Anaïs had just *done* all these things and *was* an exceptional human being.

I was alone from 1977 until 1987, ten years. I met Michael, my husband, because he had read a book of mine. Actually, he had *seen* a book, *The Woman Who Slept With Men To Take The War Out Of Them*, on a shelf in a bookstore. He'd been intrigued by the title and wanted to meet the woman who wrote the book, but he knew he was not ready to read it or, at that time, to meet the woman. Finally, he read it and, subsequently, read everything he could find of mine in print. So when I met him he knew more about my work than almost anyone alive. Through a series of "coincidences" we met through a mutual friend. Michael came to visit me two years ago when I was in the middle of a year-long retreat at my house. I invited him, partly, because he had had a very extensive Buddhist practice and been on long retreats before. That's when the relationship started and I suppose what's most remarkable about it is that he's twenty years younger than I. Certainly, I didn't expect that. It's simply amazing to me. We have a monogamous relationship because we realized that we were going to such a deep place that there was no way to share it. And we knew if we were distracted by other relationships, we couldn't be in that place with each other.

We are constantly dealing with issues of trust. Not because we don't trust each other, but because we actually trust each other so deeply that it is (I have to use the word) terrifying. Monogamy is essential to this level of intimacy.

This is a real marriage, not in the legal sense, but everything that it is in terms of THIS IS IT! You cannot leave it no matter what. You won't leave it because your souls are together and you've got to work something out. We went through considerable struggle, both of us, about how it was clear that we were connected to each other, but the package was not what we had expected. He certainly didn't expect to be monogamous with a fifty-one-year-old woman with one breast. And I didn't expect to be in love with a man twenty years younger than I. So we struggled with that.

While I can't imagine anything but monogamy with him, I can imagine very, very deep relationships with other people which aren't sexual and don't distract or undermine the intimacy between us. One can be unfaithful outside the bed, so vigilance and consciousness are necessary. There is something that happens in the sexual bond, and I think it's a pretense to say that it doesn't, that it's just having a "good time," like another form of conversation or something. It's really not true, at least for me.

I do believe that sexuality can be spiritual, can be a way to God. In that moment, the gods, the earth, the body, and the human being are connected. It is a very difficult task to learn that kind of trust, to open oneself to another human being, and also to enact as deeply as one can the reality of our interconnectedness.

During the next years in my life, I wish that I could write a book so utterly beautiful that it would make a difference. When we were in Canyon de Chelly last September and decided to get married, I had a vision that beauty comes from a Great Heart. That is what Spirit is. And there is a real desire in me to bring through, to be worthy of, this kind of vision, and to have the courage to carry it in my daily life. ■

I think it's lucky and wonderful to make it into your forties, because it takes that long to develop the skills and the philosophy that you have—which can carry you through the next forty or fifty years.

—Maxine Hong Kingston

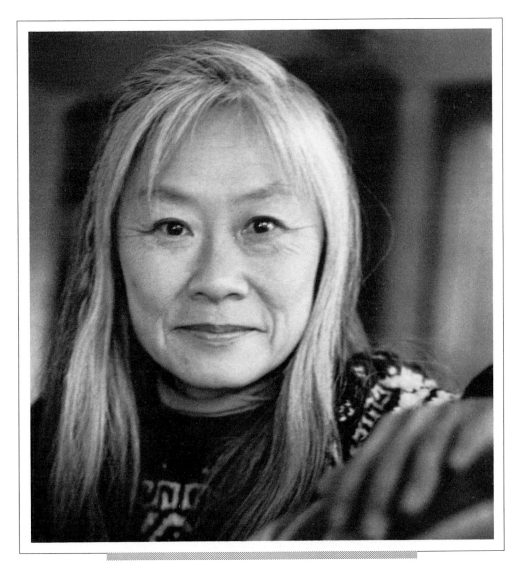

Maxine Hong Kingston

Maxine Hong Kingston is powerfully aware of the importance of role models in one's life: for the child, the student, or the middle-aged woman. The consistent strength and stability Maxine found in her artistic parents has been auspicious in understanding the oscillating tide of her own writing process. She recalls many occasions on which she "saw them lose their creativity, and then get it back," and has, subsequently, developed her own faith in the resiliency of the creative spirit.

Having had the benefit of positive parental role models, Maxine is now in the position of being an exemplary role model herself, as a professor of creative writing at the University of California, Berkeley. She sees the university system as the right place for "wise, middle-aged women." It is Maxine's goal to be an inspiration to her students, and she feels it "constantly working."

Maxine is the author of three highly acclaimed novels, *The Woman Warrior* (1976), *China Men* (1980), and *Tripmaster Monkey* (1989). She is quiescently haunted by the ghosts of her Chinese ancestors: she embodies them in her daily life and makes art from their memories. She has deep respect for the oral tradition. While curled up on a sofa, her diminutive figure half-hidden by over-sized pillows, a mane of silver framing her candid face, she spoke animatedly of her mother's "talk-stories" of Chinese legends and ancestral mysteries.

She is a woman who cares passionately about peace. We met for this interview during the Persian Gulf War, only days before the launching of the ground war. As mothers of young men in their twenties, we both held a terror in our hearts about the possibility of the U.S. government's reinstating the draft. We talked at length regarding our concern. Maxine's tearful eyes spoke expressively and her small hands gestured freely as she said: "The best protection we can give our sons so that they can take care of themselves is to have raised them with the right system of values and ethics, so that they will have learned to be men of peace."

In Maxine's current work in progress (untitled), she is integrating her commitment to pacifism with literature. In fact, she feels that this integration of personal beliefs and disparate ideas and images is what makes a woman's forties so significant. This book is different from her earlier work in that the main characters are people in her own age group who are filled with joy and upon whom she bestows a happy ending. The author believes that most American novels "are full of despair and depression."

Having experienced how visually evocative Maxine's prose is, I was not surprised when she revealed that she had been a closet artist for a good portion of her life. Maxine Hong Kingston paints images with words and creates stories through her paintings. And both reader and viewer are the richer for it.

▪ MAXINE HONG KINGSTON ▪

Looking back on my life, I see myself as a creative being from the beginning. I can't think of a time when I wasn't making up stories; I was a storyteller from the time I could talk. And as soon as I could write, I was a writer. Making up stories goes back to the time even before I found a language for what I was doing. Both of my parents are storytellers and poets, so I was always hearing stories. There was a change in my form of expression—I *spoke* the stories in Chinese, and then when I learned English I wrote them.

My parents are strong, artistic people. They have had difficult lives, but they keep their creativity alive. I've seen them lose it and then get it back. I've seen my father lose his poetry and then see it come back to him. But I guess I never have seen my mother really losing it. She's always making something, creating brand new things that no one else would ever think of. There's a constant outpouring of creativity from her. She's been doing that all along, and it never stops. It's been important to have those two people as role models.

I think we've just begun to think about the power of role models. They are important for women in their middle years because there are so few images out there; consequently, we don't know what the beauty of middle age is. But we are creating it now. We have to find the beautiful women in their forties and fifties, so that *we* can become beautiful, strong women. We must accept aging—what happens to our faces and our bodies. Not just accept, but insist that aging is beautiful, and then establish new aesthetic standards. We need to try to break through the false standards of attractiveness.

This is one reason why I kept my hair this color. There was a time when the ads said, "Wash away the ugly gray." They used the word "ugly" in ads. I just hated it! Actually, my hair was turning this color when I was quite young—I was in my twenties—so it wasn't hard to say,

"Well this is the way twenty looks," and "This is the way thirty looks." This is my political and aesthetic statement that I walk around with all the time. It's my defiance of people who say that gray is ugly. I loved it when blacks had the slogan, "Black is beautiful," and this is the same thing. I think lines around the eyes are so beautiful. I always thought so when I was young. I looked at older people and thought, "Well, I'm looking forward to getting those lines around the eyes." They make eyes so much more expressive.

In the decade of my forties, I've found that I've acted my strongest as a woman and as a creator. I have never felt such power and strength as I do now. I think this is because I've chosen a medium in which the skills get stronger and stronger as I put more time into it.

Unlike an athlete or dancer I become stronger in my craft and in my abilities as I get older. At this point in my life I have tools that are at their height. Perhaps not at their height—maybe they will be by the time I am seventy or eighty. I fully expect to live to be one hundred, because I know what tasks there are ahead of me which have to be done! There are stories and books that I have not written down yet, and I know it's going to take me many years in order to set down in words what I have to say.

The skills I have as a writer make me feel physically strong, too. I feel younger now than I did years ago. Lately I've been playing with an idea. . . there have been times in my life when I wanted to be a painter, and I painted a lot. Sometimes I want to paint again, and I wonder if I can paint now at the same height of skill that I have in my writing, or if it's necessary to go back to beginning painting. Maybe I can use the same skills that I have in writing—composition, color, imagery—all that is highly developed in my writing. Maybe those skills can transfer to painting.

When I really think wildly, I say, "Maybe I can be a dancer also." I hate the idea that ballet dancers have to start at the age of five, and it's all over by the time they're thirty. Isadora was dancing right up to the time she died. She found a way to dance that took into consideration the changes in the body.

My only regret is that I wish I'd had more confidence in art and in my abilities, so that I wouldn't have wasted so much time being scared that I couldn't make a living, or that I couldn't write or paint. I wasted too much time working at jobs just for money, and I wish I had been more creative in living. I spent much of my time being depressed, thinking that this is just the way life is—you have to get a useless job. I guess I'm talking about times when I felt lost in my art and I didn't know that I could do what I really love, and the money and all that takes care of itself. I wasted time heading in the opposite direction from where I really wanted to go. The joyful thing would have been to do my writing, my painting, to spend time with what I really loved. That's what we need to do instead of thinking what we ought to do, which is, "I ought to make a living," or "I ought to have a sensible job." I didn't need to do that. I could have gotten right to it, right to doing what I truly love. That has to do with self-knowledge; we must discover what we love and what work we are meant to do. And we need to find out as early as possible, before the world is successful at confusing us with expectations about what our roles are, and what our jobs and duties should be.

I now teach creative writing at the University of California, Berkeley, and I love it. I was a student there, and now I'm a teacher: that's just the right role for me in life.

I think teaching is right for wise middle-aged women; we have an opportunity to give the younger people our ideas and also to be role models for them, to embody ideas. I love that role. It is my goal to be an inspiration to them every time I see them, and I feel I'm reaching it constantly. In my twenties I was a teacher too, but I'm a better teacher now than I've ever been. One of my regrets in life is that there were times when I was teaching that I didn't know what I was doing. I felt lost, but I just kept going. I didn't have then what I have now to give to my students. There were times when I was in terrible despair about all kinds of things. I don't think I gave those students anything. I gave them a reading list of tragedies, and I don't think that's the best thing for young people to read.

I'm now working on a book about peace. It will integrate everything that I've learned. That is what's so important about the forties: it is the time when we begin to integrate all the years we have lived; all the disparate ideas and images come together. Living in America in the late 20th century means that you find elements of surrealism everywhere, and it is part of my task as an artist of middle-age to integrate all this and pull it together. Through this process I become a more integrated human being.

I find that my values of pacifism are coming together in my work. When I wrote *The Woman Warrior* (fifteen years ago), I was not as strong in my pacifism as I am now. When I wrote the book with "warrior" in the title, I was still working with a sense of drama that most people think of as art, where there are conflicts and confrontation and climax with violent images. It has taken many years to realize that I want to write a book where I invent a language of peace that people have not used before. Peace has really hardly been thought of for this world, and the language of peace has certainly not yet been invented. This is what I need to use my strength to work on now. Every time ideas come to me, my first thought is, "Gee, I wish somebody would do such and such." And then suddenly my next thought is, "Oh no, somebody is me!" It has

181

always been a challenge to all of us how to make a, peaceful, good world for ourselves.

My new book will bring together a variety of things, fictional and nonfictional. There has been debate among scholars whether my work is fiction or nonfiction. This book is both: truth and fantasy, reality and imagination, actual people and imaginary characters. There will be the world of theatre and the world of reality—fantasies manifested into reality. And then, of course, the greatest dream is of a pacific world juxtaposed against the reality of war. So how does one bring that together? This is what I'm working on. This is a work that a young person cannot do. It is a work of a mature, older person. But I hope it doesn't take me until I'm seventy or eighty. I hope to finish it during the next decade.

I want to show how it may be possible to be old and have a realized, human life. This is impossible for younger people to write about, even older people have not achieved it. The older, humane character has to be a communal person, someone who knows how to form family in a community. I think it's lucky and wonderful to make it into your forties, because it takes that long to develop the skills and the philosophy that you have—that can then carry you through the next forty or fifty years. There were many things during this time which helped me develop my sense of ethics. Reading is very important, because there we have available to any of us the wisdom of so many ages and cultures and people. I have found people who are strong spiritually, and it's been important to me to sit in meditation with teachers who have a strong sense of what the universe is all about.

For my fortieth birthday, a friend came from New York and gave me a big party. The whole house was filled with people. That was typical of me—I've always had lots of people around me. I felt good that I knew so many people, that I had so many friends. I felt that I must be a communal person if I have so many friends. It affirmed for me something that I've always wanted, which is that I am capable of community. And also continuity, because many of the people I know are people whom I've known forever. I have friends from high school and college. I'm bringing everybody along. I'm not someone who cuts off friendships. I like that about myself, that I have a strong sense of continuity. Those things were affirmed for me at forty.

My husband and I have been married for nearly thirty years. As I said, continuity is important to me. Since we've been married for so long, the relationship itself expresses all the ups and downs, the despair and optimism; and it changes, the way the work changes. The marriage has been long enough and deep enough, so that it comprehends all kinds of things.

Perhaps raising a son has been the most difficult thing I've done in my life, because it's actually an opportunity to create another human being. It's more than enough both to create one human, which is oneself, and then to have the responsibility of caring for another one— to make sure that he is safe, happy and alive. Reading has been such an important nourishment for me. My son is a non-reader, so I've had to wrestle with that. One way that we communicated was with chess. The years when he was being nonverbal we played chess, so I could see what kind of mind he had, and I guess he could see what kind of mind I had. But then all those moves in chess are so linear. I don't find that they have the flow and subtlety that other ways of communication have.

Being a mother is an unending task. When I look at my mother I see her still trying to shape me. It is a struggle of identity for the child to become their own person. And of course it's difficult to watch the trials that the child goes through. The parent has to experience them all over again—everything that you thought you had all figured out.

I nourish myself with meditation, psychotherapy, gardening, walking. Sometimes I take care of myself by *not* doing my writing. I take time off. To take care of myself is a brand new concept for me. I spent thirty years, maybe forty years, never having had a day off. It never occurred to me. I would just work, work, work, until I got sick, and then I'd go to bed for a few days until I could get up again. I never took a Saturday or Sunday off from anything. Actually it got so that I couldn't keep up that pace any more I was getting sick more often. I asked myself, "How do I find nourishment? Where is it coming from?" And I couldn't think of anything. I would do several things at the same time, and I didn't realize until I was older to stop and do *one* thing at a time.

One day, I was visiting my brother when my nephew was about five or six years old, and my nephew asked me to come and see his toys. So we went into his room and he showed me his toys, and then he said, "Well, where are your toys?" And I thought, "Oh, my God, I don't have any toys." That was a real Zen question: Where are my toys? What happened to them? I couldn't remember what happened to them. After that I started getting rubber stamps and I had such a good time stamping everything. It was simple for me, they were fast, and I didn't have to create them out of nothing, the way I usually do with the rest of my life and with my writing.

I think that when we are born, we have curses and gifts from our parents and our ancestors. These curses and gifts come from way back, and generation after generation, we work on them, with them. We are the latest in this line which goes back thousands of years. They are curses because there are terrible problems and hardships which are the most difficult questions of humanity, such as "why war?" and "what is love?"— very basic but difficult questions. They are also gifts, because we have the opportunity to come up with the most beautiful answers. And I see our ancestors as trying to come up with answers, sometimes failing and sometimes succeeding. To me success means effectiveness in the world, that I am able to carry my ideas and values into the world— that I am able to change it in positive ways. Success means to be able to create beautiful things in the world, to make the world more beautiful, and to be able to communicate with it. Our ancestors have succeeded and stayed alive to the extent that we are here, and we have one more chance to do it right. ∎

Perhaps this is the message (more than any other) I'd like to give to the world (especially to Americans, who are so easily bored and run around looking for anything new): that you stay with something because that's how you deepen your life; otherwise, you are always on the surface.

—Natalie Goldberg

Natalie Goldberg

Feeling lost on a dirt road six miles northwest of Taos, New Mexico, I headed for the flailing arms of a tall, lean, tanned woman in cutoffs, who was in the process of planting juniper trees next to neat rows of lettuce and broccoli in her spacious front garden. Natalie Goldberg greeted me with a bright smile and led me into her home. She lives alone in a one-room, solar-heated shelter, built right into and up against the raw sienna-colored clay soil. Peaceful, nurturing, protective, it was quiet enough inside to imagine the pulse/heartbeat of the earth, like a child nestled against her mother's breast.

Natalie prepared Sunday breakfast and as we shared French toast, we also shared life stories. She seemed to have as many questions for me as I had for her. We looked at slides of her watercolors which were definitely and defiantly hers—a dash of Henry Miller and Marc Chagall—with primary-colored, anthropomorphized everyday objects dancing to an unheard but clearly felt pied piper's tune. They possessed all the personality and genuineness inherent to Natalie, the woman, and to Natalie, the writer.

That morning, prior to my arrival, there had been a call of encouragement from fellow-writer Erica Jong, praising the importance of and wishing all success for Natalie's new book. Asked how her new celebrity status is affecting her, Natalie replied with a wide grin: "I love it!" To illustrate the scope of this public recognition, she recalled a friend, who, upon hearing the messages on Natalie's telephone answering machine, joked: "Nat, you don't just get messages, you get, 'Oh, Natalie, I love your work and I love you!'" She particularly enjoys the correspondence from blue-collar workers, people she never thought would respond to her book.

This national attention is caused by *Writing Down the Bones, Freeing the Writer Within*. The title instantly makes sense: writing as a means to express the bare essentials, one's true authenticity. This Zen-like (in perspective and execution) book could have just as easily been called: *Using Writing as a Way to Help You Penetrate Your Life and Become Sane*. Discipline is the key. Any discipline will do, will bring you to a place of sanity, or centeredness, or, if you will, happiness. Writing, as with any committed act, any discipline, is a path to personal depth and truth. As a practicing Zen Buddhist for fifteen years, Natalie is learning to make writing and life her practice.

Some books are so open and comfortable with themselves that they automatically share their ease with the reader. Before I had even finished the book, I was on the phone ready for an interview with Natalie. I didn't reach her at first, as she was on a ten-day retreat in Minnesota, her previous, long-term residence. Two weeks later, I gave myself a gift by calling her exactly on my birthday. It was a sentimental thing to do and Natalie shared my enjoyment in the specialness of the day and moment.

During the course of the interview, she was completely and refreshingly straightforward yet unpredictable in her responses. Questions which might have been profound or, at least, thought-provoking to others were either of little importance or non-applicable to her.

Later that afternoon, when we had completed our interview and were saying our good-byes, Natalie's parting advice was: "Write your book; it will change your life." As I write this, a small hand-made, hand-burnished clay pot made by a Taos Pueblo Native American sits on my desk in front of me, a gift from Natalie. It is a completely sensual remembrance of New Mexico in the summer: the same burnt umber color, the same smell and feel of the earth on her mesa. I rub it, as if, by so doing, my writing will be magical and my life will be blessed. And I imagine Natalie in her earthen home: secure, happy in her solitude, writing.

I was raised in a very Jewish family and my vision of the world was their vision. I picked a college which had both law and medical schools; my mother said that I could meet a lawyer or a doctor there. I listened to her, I followed everything my mother said. When I graduated from college and wasn't getting married, that script was done; I realized I could create my own life.

Since then my whole life has been different! I've been married and divorced—I don't even think about marriage now. I'm a deeply committed Buddhist; a deeply committed writer. I live on a mesa six miles from town, away from people. I was never brought up to do any of that. When I stepped out, I *totally* stepped out. I'm very, very different. My entire life is different from what I was brought up to be.

These last two years since I moved back to Taos, I don't have a great need for family any more, but I have an enormous number of friends, and I see my students and the people who work with me as being my family. I've created my own family, because the early vision I had of family wouldn't allow me to be the Natalie Goldberg I am now.

Until recently I thought I might have children, but lately my life is opening in new ways and I find myself only in love with children. You need to have a connection with the next generation. I spend time with my friends' kids and I always say, jokingly: "In five years I'll be ready to have kids." But I'll be forty-five and probably won't want them then. Life hasn't taken me that way. My work is much bigger, my *work* is my children and I also feel that I've been parenting myself for many years.

My friends tease me—I'll totally be into jogging for a year then drop it. Right now, I'm taking horseback riding lessons. I completely get into something for a while and it enriches my life. But Buddhism and writing are the two things I've always stayed with. I've used them to penetrate my life and I hope they will stay with me. I can't imagine them not, though the outside form might change.

Joking recently with my friend, Kate Green, I said, "You know, Kate, in ten years I think I'm going to stop writing." She said, "Oh yeah, what are you going to do?" I said, "I think I'm gonna go into politics!" She teased, "Mayor of Taos? We'll go into a restaurant and the host will ask, 'Would you like the writing or the non-writing section?'!"

To me creativity means having a fresh approach to something and, if you do, then you try to be present in your life and in whatever you do. So when I write I try to be in the moment, not in my stale thoughts. I keep my hand going. When I paint, I sit in front of a tree and become one with the tree—it's very simple. I don't believe that some people are creative and some aren't; I don't even think of creativity. I just try to be present.

Recently I had an argument with a friend; we were really fighting. I hated her and she hated me. While we were right in the middle of it, the thought popped up in my head: "O.K., Nat, how can you create peace here? What are you willing to do to create an opening for communication?" I tried different things and finally one of them worked. *That's* what creative is: in the midst of my hating her and being closed down, my deeper commitment was to create peace. My effort made me feel very autonomous, in control of my feelings: they weren't ruling me.

I don't think that much about spirituality. I had an awakening when I was twenty-six years old. All I had wanted to do was to sit and become friends with my own mind. Then I got rolfed, and after my first session the practitioner said that I protected myself in the heart. After the rolfing, I experienced the Garden of Eden inside me. It was a deep experience. This was fifteen years ago and it has held strong.

Buddhism is a good vehicle: it's a method, a path that takes me to

191

the Truth. There are many paths, but I think it's important to take one and stay with it. One of the things about the New Age that is very sad to me is that everyone runs around trying this and trying that. Finally, I think you have to commit yourself to something (whether you love it or hate it) and stay with it under all circumstances.

I met with Marianne Grossman, a brilliant woman, who is the book editor for the St. Paul Pioneer Press. She told me that she's been studying the New Age. She said what scares her is that people take a little from this and a little from that, everything that they *like*. But ultimately, it's like marriage: sometimes you hate your husband, but that doesn't matter because below that anger there must be some kind of commitment. Whether you hate or love something, you stay with it. That's why I've stayed with Buddhism. I've committed myself to it: to the practice and to *staying* with it. It's true of writing, too. There are days when I think: "What the hell did I choose here?" But it doesn't matter whether I love it or hate it, I'm a writer and I take it on.

So my definition of spirituality is: "Shut up and do your work and stay with it under all circumstances." Perhaps this is the message (more than any other) I'd like to give to the world (especially to Americans, who are so easily bored and run around looking for anything new): stay with something because that's how you *deepen* your life; otherwise, you are always on the surface. But I think it's as Suzuki Roshi said: "When you do something, do it completely!", so that it burns completely and there is nothing left.

I was divorced six years ago. My husband and I competed a lot and I decided: "O.K. I can't have you, I can't have love, but I'm going to have my writing." So I really protected my art and also I really grieved. For three years my heart wasn't available. Now I'm beginning to open again. My work is so safe and O.K. that I can take care of other areas in my life.

To have an intimate relationship is presently the most challenging area in my life. That's where I'm focusing; that's what I'm trying to understand. I'm giving energy to it; I care. The word *love* has been thrown around so much. I guess love is the willingness to accept things and people as they are, having compassion for people and for all things. I certainly have a lot of love, but I watch how some of my love gets perverted and then suddenly becomes desire—suddenly becomes something else that isn't love at all. I become angry and try to manipulate, and at that point love dies. I've done all kinds of things—in Buddhism they call it the three poisons of ego: passion, aggression and ignorance. We either want to pull something toward us, push it away or numb out.

I'm always examining things, trying to figure out the world—not analytically, but with my heart. I don't really know how I know things, but it doesn't come from the intellect. It doesn't come from my brain—I know everything through my belly. I go back to "beginner's mind." I get very dumb—I go to the essential things—that's how I examine life. I'm so curious. I want to understand the world. Sometimes I think too much and I have to remember that there is another reality out there. I have a tremendous imagination. We could walk into a cafe and it's not just *a* cafe, it's the *greatest* cafe in America. While I'm very enthusiastic, I also have to remember the ordinariness of things: that it's also just a salt shaker and it shakes salt.

I don't know if there is much of a "purpose" for life, but in the face of no purpose we must acknowledge the suffering and help heal it. So how do you do that without being a do-gooder? You learn about it in yourself and heal it in yourself. I think that helps the world.

I think the purpose of *my* life is to wake up! To wake up and deepen and understand how I can create peace between me and another person, between me and the chair, between me and myself, between me and society.

Success means balancing out being successful in the world and not getting caught up or tossed away by it. Success to me is being able to handle it and not getting turned around by believing other people's ideas about who I am—being able to keep it in balance and keep my life in balance.

I've gotten older. On one level I don't care. On another level I think: "God, I had such a great body when I was young," but I didn't appreciate it. I think I've gotten prettier, I think I'm stronger, I have more endurance. I rather hope I won't look too bad at fifty—that my muscles won't be falling to my knees!

I have an image of living to be very old. My grandparents both died in their nineties. I think one of our practices is to realize that *every moment we die and come alive again* and at one point we die in this world to come alive someplace else. I think it makes your life very vital *right now*. I don't know when I'll die—I've died many times—I'm not the same Natalie Goldberg that I was a year ago.

One of the most important things I've learned is not to always believe my emotions, not to give them so much credence. And that's odd, because we learn in therapy that anger is important—that other emotions are important; but there is the next step where they are also not everything—they are not solid. Life is impermanent; you can't hold on to anything.

I feel fulfilled. I have work that matters to me—work that is important. I love doing my workshops. I love my house on the mesa; I am totally happy to be here. I like that I can travel and that my time is my own. I can choose what I want to do and what I don't want to do, so I feel great freedom. I have friends whom I deeply love. But there is something beyond all that which makes me happy. . . it's like I wake up singing.

I used to get the blues, but I just burned through somehow. There is some bottom line of contentment or incredible satisfaction that I have. I don't know if it's my Buddhist practice, but it *is* my spiritual life and my gratitude for my life. Life is a gift and I am *receiving* it now. I'm noticing it and receiving it. I feel that the earth is supporting me. ■

Because I was drinking when I turned forty, I didn't feel that turn which many women feel when they hit their late thirties— they know forty is approaching and they feel their finitude.

—Linda Leonard

Linda Leonard

I had been attempting to meet with Linda Leonard for more than a year. On sabbatical from her practice as a Jungian analyst in San Francisco, she went to the majestic Rocky Mountains in Colorado. There she hoped to take the time and make the space to go deeper into herself in order to get a perspective on what had happened to her in her forties, and, in the Heideggerian sense, to get a glimpse of what the future was bringing toward her. It was difficult to coordinate our schedules due to her rigorous lecturing tour on a national and international circuit and a disciplined writing life (focusing on a new project concerning the mystical feminine), whenever she was at home. We finally set a date the week before Christmas when Linda would be visiting the San Francisco Bay Area.

On the appointed day I met her at a favorite book store, Black Oak, in North Berkeley. After café au lait at Chez Panisse, we arrived at my house where I had been preparing a hearty, rich winter stew, ossobuco, for two days. Our discussion ran late into the night, and we arose early the next morning to continue the interview as we walked the appropriately named trail, "Inspiration Point." I appreciated the fact that she not only loves cinema as much as I do, but is especially drawn to the most obscure—even bizarre—foreign films just as I am.

We reviewed the impact of our favorite directors: Fassbinder, Bergman, Roeg, Truffaut, Ozu, Scorsese, and recounted endless movie experiences comparing what their characters meant to each of us: how we identified them as fictional representations of our own lives, in particular, and of the human condition, in general.

Having read in depth two of her three published books I felt as if I already knew this woman through the raw exposure of her life in her writing. Linda scrutinizes her existence and her psyche as if she were a laboratory scientist who has discovered a method for dissecting the soul. She is her own experiment—testing every experience and every emotion, always with a compassionate heart. Her willingness to share herself on the most personal level and publicly reveal her darkest fears and aversions make the disclosure of her life as an alcoholic now in recovery a hopeful revelation to the reader—even if the reader, herself, is not an alcoholic. Telling one's story, as a method of personal catharsis and as a means of teaching others, is as old as human memory. I was drawn by her authenticity. She possesses the admirable combination of self-esteem and humility, and I identified with her troubled voyage through a difficult life.

More than a decade before reading *Witness to the Fire*, Linda's third book, I had executed a body of about a dozen larger-than-life sized oil paintings which I called *The Demon Lover* Series. Working on these canvases had been an experience in exorcising childhood and adolescent traumas which had been caused by both one abusive parent and another alcoholic parent, and by coerced participation in organized religion. Art had been my attempt to come to terms with my womanhood. The startling and haunting imagery I used in these pieces (some of which appeared to me in dreams) evoked archetypal characterizations, I have since discovered through research, which are found trans-culturally. In *Witness to the Fire* I found, virtually, a compendium or handbook which aided me in understanding how my phantoms reflected universally recognized inner figures of the human psyche. *Witness to the Fire* is about the journey of transformation from the bondage of addiction to a life of meaning and creativity. Through the paradigms of existential philosophy, Jungian psychology, and literary analysis, Linda Leonard explores the relationship between addiction and creativity, and the slow, arduous process of recovery through a twelve step program.

Using primarily her own personal history—in particular, her fight to save herself from the destruction of alcoholism—Linda provides readers with comfort through the fact that someone has gone through exactly what they feel—and survived. The sources of addictions vary—alcohol, drugs, food, sex, money, power—but the symptoms and manifestations, the overwhelming sense of personal despair remain the same in each addict.

According to Linda, by finally accepting the existential dilemma that after you have recognized that there is seemingly no purpose in life, you still must daily renew your commitment to a faith in something greater than yourself. Then a human being can begin to come to terms with herself and live a life of content and fulfillment. Her books are maps of how to do this—how she did it, herself. She is a cartographer of the soul, exploring the geology of the psyche.

As a scholar and intellectual who was trained at the Jung Institute in

Zurich, Linda has a kind of emotional and psychological depth that pervades her writing. And a profound sense of spiritual awareness permeates her professional work and her personal life. She brings an intelligence and seriousness to the usually simplistically empty pop psychology and New Ageism found rampant in bookstores and in the media. I believe that this is due to the fact that behind every theory Linda devises there lies the pain of her personal experience.

According to Goethe:

> Talent alone cannot make a writer.
> There must be a [wo]man behind
> the book.

I always wanted to be a writer, so I studied journalism in college at Temple University. I got a job on a daily newspaper in Colorado, and worked as a reporter for a few years. I wanted to help people—to offer a service—and I think that desire existed because I came from a dysfunctional family that was in great pain. I thought of helping people through journalism but soon realized that I didn't have the kind of depth of knowledge that I wanted in my writing. So I decided to go to graduate school and major in philosophy. Literature would have been my preference, but I figured I could do literature on my own. However, after trying to read Kierkegaard, I realized I couldn't do philosophy on my own.

"What is the meaning of life?" was my main question. It always was and remains my quest even today. When I got into philosophy, I found that most of the philosophers were not interested in that question and didn't even think it was valid philosophically. Philosophy seemed to be extremely rational and analytic . . . it seemed to exclude who I was as a person, and especially who I was as a woman. I was told by my professors that I shouldn't go on in philosophy in graduate school. Philosophy felt totally foreign to me and I thought I would stop. But during my final semester a woman was hired in the philosophy department and she taught a course in the philosophy of literature and existentialism. I found that the existentialists were the ones who were asking the same questions about the meaning of life: what does it mean to be human here and now, today, with all the feelings that you have as a person, and how does that affect your relationships with other people, your relationship with society, and your relationship with the cosmos as a whole?

Heidegger was my major influence. Camus, Kafka, Tolstoy, Rilke, Hesse, and especially Dostoevsky were the primary literary influences. In philosophy, there was Kierkegaard and Nietsche—also Buber and

Tillich to some extent, but particularly Heidegger, because he was questioning the same issues I was concerned with: death and guilt (I felt a great deal of guilt and shame coming from the family that I grew up in). He was asking questions about conscience and authenticity—how do you lead an authentic life? I was drawn to his images of nature. He is a philosopher who wrote from a hut which was in a clearing just below the forest line on a mountain. He was connected with nature, and I was too. Heidegger also dialogued with poets whom I loved. He really spoke to me.

Existentialism puts the focus on your daily existence, the meaning of your actions, the meaning of your choices. It focuses on the fact that you have freedom and responsibility about the way you lead your life.

This is also what the twelve-step programs do. Maybe you're doing it from the viewpoint of hoping to get through a particular addiction, but it's a very existential process, the twelve steps.

Focusing on the existentialists has helped me to see the world as a more humane place. I see many films and read a good deal of literature and poetry and enjoy the ballet, opera, and theatre. Every time I go to a film, if it's a good film, or read a good book, it puts me back into that place where I look at my own life and see what choices I'm making, where I have to empathize with someone else, and how I deal with those kinds of conflicts. I experience through all the artistic mediums what it means to be human. It seems that I choose to confront myself via art with the struggle of life. I see that as the crux of the existential approach.

The breakthrough in existential philosophy was the focus on feelings and the emotions—on what was important to the individual's personal life. Before the advent of existentialism, the personal perspective and the feminine had been disregarded—you needed to take a totally objective view of things. But existentialists came along and declared that there was no way to take a totally objective view of things because you are always in a situation; whenever you ask a question the questioner is part of the question that they are asking. In other words, the viewer affects the outcome and is part of the whole process; the subject and object are not separated. I think that is naturally a feminine way of looking at things.

The philosophers who were atheistic didn't attract me because I had a connection with something larger than myself. I loved Simone de Beauvoir, though, and simply hungered for her early autobiographies. She was certainly influential to me as a woman who was living her own life. I knew I was a different kind of person, but I hungered to find out about women (and it was hard to do in those days): women's psychology, the female psyche, what helped women in their lives, what were their values. What could they contribute, and how did they come to be able to contribute? I was terribly involved with those questions. But there weren't many women writing whom I had discovered. Anaïs Nin also influenced me. And reading Ayn Rand helped me get away from a dysfunctional family situation that was parasitic, though I disagreed with her politics.

Coming from a dysfunctional family which was both alcoholic and codependent, I now understand that the dark, raw pain of wounds were exposed all the time. I grew up with those wounds, with what Jung would call the shadow; my family was basically a shadow family. And so, the problem of evil immediately confronted me. The shadow is the part of reality, or the part of yourself, that is unconscious, that you as the conscious person haven't even recognized or have rejected. It is something either in the individual, the family, or the society that's usually repressed or suppressed. It's difficult to deal with.

My family was a shadow family, in the sense that we tried to hide the fact that my father was an alcoholic. I even tried to hide it from my friends. As a teenager I developed the logos side of my being, the intellectual side, to help shield me from all the violence that was going on in my family—all the dark and difficult, nightmarish kinds of things that were happening. Because I lived in that situation, I was always confronted with questions about justice and suffering and the problem of evil.

I grew up in a family where the women were strong. My mother's mother lived with my family and basically did the housework, while my mother supported the family as a typist in a department store on minimum wage. We were poor and it was not an intellectual family, but my grandmother spent much of her time reading poetry to me and helping me with Latin and my other studies. She loved nature, poetry, and Thoreau and Emerson and the other transcendental philosophers, which she had read on her own. She had been raised as a simple farm girl, but she imbued me with a deep love and appreciation of nature. No one in my family had graduated from high school, but my father and grandmother instilled in me a love of learning, and encouraged an education. So I had a positive directive in that way. My mother was and is a very grounded and practical person. She gave me a good sense of embodiment and how to survive in difficult situations. She is street wise.

I remember thinking that school was the best place for me because it seemed safe. I had many questions about life, but I pretty much lived alone with those questions. And occasionally I'd read something in a book that would help me. That's probably where the desire to write came from. By the time I was in my early twenties I was working as a journalist, hoping to raise these questions in some fashion and explore the meaning of life. But I soon discovered that newspapers don't do that. I felt that I lacked the kind of knowledge you get from studying the humanities, and that if I were to read more novels I would understand what it means to be human, because novelists write from the human parts of themselves. Philosophers were also exploring deeply. Actually, philosophy means love of wisdom. And I wanted wisdom.

I went to the Jung Institute in Zurich because I wanted to understand the inner workings of an individual. I understood quite a bit generally by the time I was through with philosophy, but I wanted to see what happens in an individual's psyche. In Zurich I became an analyst in order to work intimately with people, learning how to work with dreams and symbolic material.

Understanding the dream life—how it affects a person's life, how it can change a person's life, and how someone can grow by comprehending how their dreams and universal patterns operate in their life—was fascinating to me.

When I received my diploma from the Jung Institute I returned to the United States and taught for about six years. During this time my father died, and after his death I had many dreams in which I saw clearly that I was to understand everything I could about the father complex. I then felt an urge to write about the father-daughter relationship, because of my own wound with my father. Because he died before I was able to reconcile with him, I felt an enormous amount of guilt and sorrow. I also recognized that my unresolved relationship with him was affecting all my other relationships. All of this was the impetus to begin writing *The Wounded Woman*.

I didn't know what I would put in the book, but gradually it revealed itself. Primarily, writing that book helped me to forgive my father and to have compassion for him. But in the process of writing it I discovered different patterns and ways that a woman's life could take if she had an injured relationship with her father, who was, himself, injured. I learned about and healed myself by writing this book. The method I used was to turn to literature and then describe various characters with whom I identified.

I began with the simple idea that there are two opposing tendencies in the female: one who wants to stay the girl, the eternal girl (called *puella* in Latin), and the armored amazon, who has the masculine armor to shield herself, but also has the vulnerable girl inside. These are two opposites, both of which I felt existed within myself, and within every woman. However, one was usually predominant, while the other remained more in shadow and not so recognized. I studied it from the perspective of a woman's experience. I saw these patterns in other women, in clients and friends, and I described them. I hoped that the end of the book would be the point where I could redeem the father principle in myself.

The entire process had been merely to get me to return to my own feminine center, and an important part of writing the book for me was to tell my own story of my relationship between my father and myself. I feel that this is so important to the feminine principle that women tell their stories. But ten years ago publishers didn't want to hear about women's personal emotional experiences. So I received forty-two rejections on my book. The tendency is to give up when you're rejected. But for some reason I didn't. I think I had a certain sense of destiny about this book and continued to struggle through all those rejections. I stuck to what I believed in. Finally, when the book came out it was very successful (and is now translated into twelve languages around the globe). For the second time since my experience with discrimination in graduate school, I was again dealing with the patriarchy. It was important for me to tell the story of my growing up in an alcoholic family. Now people realize the need for such stories, but at the time there was no precedent.

The idea of having children was an open question for me, which I thought I would deal with in my thirties. I'd been married in my twenties and had gotten a divorce after I returned from Zurich. By the time I reached my thirties, when I was thinking of having children, I was out of any relationship. I wanted to have children, although that wasn't my major orientation (contributing something to the development of humans in society was always my major focus). However, there wasn't an available partner. When I passed into my forties, it became less and less likely that I would have children, and I was somewhat resolved to it. But when I hit menopause in my late forties, the reality that I definitely would not have children—because you always think there is still time, or at least I did—really came upon me. And then I felt quite a bit of grief.

On the other hand, I thought, perhaps my destiny was to write these books. I had a very strong sense of that. Maybe I could have done both, I don't know—it's a paradox. It's something I've missed out on in this life.

I've been free to do certain things that I couldn't have done if I'd had children. But as I get older, it seems to be more of a loss.

I didn't start drinking until I was thirty, when I moved to Europe, where there was a lifestyle of daily drinking. I just let myself go into a Dionysian lifestyle. In some ways I wish that I hadn't had to follow that path. But in a way it *was* my path, because that's what I've been writing about. One thing you learn in dealing with addictions in twelve-step programs is that you can't really say, "If only I hadn't done this, or done that." You have to start where you are. That's also existential. You start where you are, and then you deal with that situation. So I try to approach things that way. I have a tendency, as an addict, to say "If only

I hadn't . . ." But that's not the way life works; I think we have to deal with whatever comes up each day.

I feel that there was probably some meaning in the fact that I was born into a family of addicts, where practically all the men were alcoholics and almost all the women married alcoholics. It is a family that was rampant with addiction. I suppose that was one of my tasks: to transform that process that my father wasn't able to transform, nor his father, nor my mother, because she was co-dependent. So it fell on me, and the way I did that was through the process of first becoming a philosopher, then a therapist, then a writer. I now see it as a path of knowledge I had to take.

Because I was drinking when I turned forty, I didn't feel that turn which many woman feel when they hit their late thirties. They know forty is approaching and they feel their finitude, particularly if they haven't had children. But even if they have, they may still feel a certain loss. So I didn't really feel the things that most people feel around forty until I hit my late forties, when I stopped drinking.

Many significant things happened to me during my forties: I came into my own as a Jungian analyst, I was established, I'd already been a philosophy teacher, and I'd had a tenured position, which I gave up to go into practice fulltime. My first two books, *The Wounded Woman*, and *On the Way to the Wedding,* were published and I started my third book, *Witness to the Fire*. It was a decade of incredible transformation and creativity. I think what really happened in my forties was that all my previous delving into the depths, trying to understand the meaning of existence began to fall into place; and I began to see parallels and make analogies.

During this time I was faced with the fact that I had a serious drinking problem. Part of my purpose in writing *The Wounded Woman* was also, hopefully, to transform the drinking into normal social drinking. By the time I finished the book I knew that wasn't going to happen, and that I would have to give up drinking, entirely. But I found it difficult to do that; I tried to do it on my own for about two or three years but wasn't successful. Finally, I had a series of serious relapses and was told that if I didn't stop drinking I would either die or go mad due to the Korsakov syndrome.

That really scared me, so at that point I went into the Twelve Steps, and that's when I started my recovery process—when I was in my forties. I found a whole new life in that process of recovery. That's when I started my second book, *On the Way to the Wedding*, and realized I could write without drinking.

The book is about the sacred marriage with the Divine. It's probably what I always felt but was able to experience much more consciously, and maybe existentially, in the process of recovery, because I knew that something greater than myself had to be present in order for me to stop drinking. It was a miracle. And I knew that. I felt at a deep level, first the dark night of the soul, and then the fact that something Higher stepped in and helped me. I had to be humbled before I could turn toward the Divine of my own free will and ask for help. This second book came out of that experience of the descent and also the knowledge that it was possible to receive help and experience the Divine in a new way. *On the Way to Wedding* was also a celebration for me which coincided with my finally being able to sustain a meaningful, long-term, committed relationship. That was a gift which was given to me.

My third book, *Witness to the Fire*, was an attempt to understand the psychological implications of addiction, and also what the philosphical aspects were in addiction. I turned to the existentialists to do that—to the works of writers who were addicts and who were describing inner characters of addiction. Writing that book helped me work through all those figures in myself; it also helped me to see how the Twelve Steps was itself a process of creation, paralleling the creative process, and why it worked, that it actually was a universal process.

I felt that humans can go in a creative direction or a destructive direction. The destructive direction would be addiction. There is a fundamental choice at some point. Addiction often covers up the creative because the poet or artist is afraid to face the terror, all the work and struggle that is inherent in the creative process. When I was in the detox center, I woke up in terror and thought, "I am in the dark night of the soul," but the words of the Christian mystic, St. John of the Cross, came to me. He said, "The night darkens the soul but only to illumine it." So I came to believe that there is a parallel between the addictive process and what Jung calls the descent into the unconscious, of the night sea journey.

This is what all the mystics call the dark night of the soul, which is something I knew that writers and creative people also experience; they make a descent into the unknown. I had already done that in writing *The Wounded Woman*, and I had studied the process in other writers, particularly in the poet, Rainer Maria Rilke, whose work I'd used in my Jungian thesis called, "Rilke and the Individuation Process." So I knew that they were similar processes, and I wanted to understand how they worked. I wanted to understand the differences between the person who remains an addict and the person who is an addict but goes into recovery. I also wanted to understand the dynamic of the creative person who makes the descent and brings back a creation.

Many creative people have addictive problems, but they resist giving up their addictions because they are afraid they will lose their creative life. Using my experiences as a Jungian analyst, as an existential philosopher, and as an alcoholic, I hoped that by writing I would simultaneously heal that wound in myself and make a contribution to others. So that was my urge—those were some of my motivations in writing the book.

Initially I went to the dictionary and looked up the meaning of the word "addiction." I found that it meant "to deliver yourself over," but also "to devote yourself to something." It didn't always have a perjorative meaning. That was when I realized that there was a turning point when you could deliver yourself over to the negative addictive direction. I saw the archetypal figure behind that being what I call the demon lover. This has been discussed down through the ages by various poets and artists. The energy behind turning toward a positive creative direction is known as the creative daimon, which people like Rilke, Yeats, and many other artists have described as the indwelling creative spirit within themselves which caused them to create, so that they *must* create. They feel destined to create. The creative daimon holds the tension of the choice between the divine and the diabolic.

That same energy is what Jung talks about in the individuation process: that every individual has within themselves the potential to be who they are in the fullest possible way. To me, that is in some ways the existential crux as well, because each individual is faced with the responsibility to choose either a creative or a destructive direction.

It really is a matter of life and death, whether you are talking about physical death, spiritual annihilation, or a life that has meaning. I had to make the choice. And I continue to make it every day and in some ways every single moment. Everyone does. To stop drinking was one of the most difficult things—perhaps *the* most difficult thing—I've had to do in my life.

It was harder than writing books, harder than getting any degree, harder than climbing Mt. Kilimanjaro. But now I feel it's a great gift not to drink. The gift of recovery and being able to turn more fully toward the creative was one of the greatest things that has ever happened to me.

The addictive modes in society, and in an individual, are abusive to the gentle, mystical feminine element. When an addiction takes over, you lose gentleness and vulnerability. When it finally takes over you become cold and deadened; and you are driven by a hard, cold master. Finally it feels demonic. In some ways it is like a rape by an outside influence; it slowly begins to take over your life. Healing the divisive aspects within ourselves, and within our society, will help to bring about the sacred marriage . . . between heaven and earth, between the masculine and feminine that I describe in *On the Way to the Wedding*.

The idea of aging has been difficult for me. I was faced with finitude and limitations that I needed to accept. I don't know that I've totally accepted them—it's a continuing process. But aging has also brought with it an awareness that my time is shortening, and that I want to contribute as much as I can now, from this place. I want to bring the things that I've learned out into the world, even more than I already have. I feel more responsibility to the world. At the end of my forties I took a sabbatical to get the time and space to go deeper in myself—to get the perspective of what happened in my forties since I stopped drinking—and also to get a perspective of where I'm going. I needed a lot of space, and so I went to the mountains. Hiking and cross-country skiing help me to center myself. They give me a sense of strength, both physically and psychically; and when I do these things I feel related to the Divine. Writing also does that for me, and dialogue with friends is essential. So I find that if I don't write and I don't hike, I get out of touch, off-center; but when I do those things I get connected with where I need to be.

I feel more integrated; most of the time I feel more at ease with myself and with other people. Because I feel more joy, I also feel more pain, the pain of wounding. Now I see the dark night of the soul as a cycle, like the seasons, that we all go through. I even see it as a daily cycle and go through it without as much resistance as before. ■

> *It costs so much to be a full human being that there are very few who have the love and courage to pay the price. One has to abandon altogether the search for security and reach out to the risk of living with both arms. One has to embrace life like a lover.*
>
> —Morris West

The author welcomes the personal stories of mid-life transition and transformation from readers of *Coming into Our Fullness*. Please send correspondence to: Cathleen Rountree, P.O. Box 552, Aptos, CA 95001.

The Crossing Press publishes a number of books of special interest to women. For a complete catalog please call toll-free 1-800-777-1048.